# Country
## in the City

# Country in the CITY

## Relaxed Style for Modern Living

Liz Bauwens &
Alexandra Campbell

Photography by Simon Brown

CICO BOOKS

London

To my parents and Lois, Milo and Finn

To David, Frederick and Rosalind

First published in Great Britain in 2001 by Cima Books Ltd
32 Great Sutton Street
London EC1V 0NB

This paperback edition published in 2003

10 9 8 7 6 5 4 3 2 1

A CIP catalogue record for this book is available from the British Library

ISBN 1 903116 80 5

Photography by Simon Brown
Designed by David Fordham
Edited by Mary Lambert

Typeset by MATS, Southend-on-Sea, Essex
Reproduction by Saffron Reprographics, London
Printed and bound in Singapore by Tien Wah Press

# CONTENTS

# INTRODUCTION

EVERYONE HAS A DREAM of the perfect country house: a beautiful, warm and welcoming place with a sense of comfort and style that comes naturally. The word 'country' evokes a timeless simplicity, where classic form is married to a soft decorative feel, where colour and pattern are used informally and where light and space are at the very heart of every room.

In an increasingly international world, it is also the countryside that retains individual characteristics, crafts and designs, while cities the world over share many of the same global brands and fashions. With the re-introduction of colour and pattern to interior design and the perennial popularity of natural materials, contemporary country style offers all homes a simple, accessible vision of stylish living, which is also supremely comfortable – often understated, but immediately appreciated. It can be frustrating to thumb through a book of beautiful country interiors and see that so many of the effects are due to the architecture or location of the houses. What *Country in the City* aims to do is to take the elements of country style – individuality, natural materials, soft, decorative patterns, comfort, light and space – and re-interpret them for any interior today – from a small coastal cottage or an apartment in the tallest tower block.

These looks work in all kinds of houses, conversions, maisonettes and apartments. The houses featured are real homes that are lived in, and their decorative schemes have evolved naturally rather than having been artificially 'designed'. All are outstandingly successful interiors, yet none were created with unlimited budgets. Each scheme has a realistic mix of attention to quality and detail, money-saving choices and the occasional dash of extravagance to create the ultimate in stylish, chic living.

# Country
# KITCHENS

WARMTH AND WELCOME ARE THE WORDS THAT DEFINE A COUNTRY KITCHEN, BUT THE CASUAL MIX OF OLD AND NEW, ALONG WITH A SENSE OF LIGHT AND SPACE, CAN BE ACHIEVED IN COUNTRY, TOWN OR CITY HOMES. CHOOSE YOUR COLOUR SCHEMES FROM THE GARDEN OUTSIDE — WHETHER IT'S A WINDOW BOX OR A VISTA OF ROLLING FIELDS — AND USE TACTILE NATURAL WOOD AND EARTHY CERAMICS.

# SHAKER

RIGHT: The red cotton
checked curtains add some
visual warmth to the
room; without them, a
cool scheme of green,
blue and white would be
too austere.

LEFT: The kitchen table is made from
maple, and copied from one in Hancock
Shaker Village in Massachusetts, so the
kitchen worktops are also maple to
match, because mixing light and dark
woods in the same room destroys
visual continuity.

THE COUNTRY KITCHEN STANDS for a warm welcome and good food – a place where
friends and family can relax and enjoy themselves. Visually, those elements translate
into simple, timeless designs, natural woods, an inviting atmosphere of sunlight pouring
through the window and cheerful, innocent patterns. There is nothing pretentious about
the country kitchen, and yet it's too easy to lose the concept in a muddle of clutter.
That is why the Shaker fashion, with its formula of 'beauty based on utility', has become
a classic blueprint for the style. This city basement was the prototype design for Shaker
Kitchens, and was created by Liz Shirley of the Shaker Shop in London.

    She first had to overcome a problem that many homes have – a room with poor natural
light. She removed a dividing wall between it and another room to increase the sense of
light and space, but, even so, the kitchen's design and the colour scheme had to be chosen.

11

LEFT: The sink and things related to wet activities, such as dishwashers or washing machines, are in a scullery area just off the main kitchen to free up living space – a useful trick if you only have a small utility room off the kitchen. The maple 'heart' breadboards come from The Shaker Shop.

BELOW: Decorative detail was always plain and simple on all Shaker items. But there is a beauty in its simplicity, here the heart pattern used on the breadboards repeats on the serviettes (BOTTOM).

## WOODS, PAINTED OR NATURAL?

MOST PEOPLE HAVE ONE or two things that travel with them from house to house. For Liz Shirley, this was an old Victorian pine dresser and an Aga kitchen range. The kitchen was then 'built round' these two starting points. The maple kitchen table was copied from one in Hancock Shaker Village, Massachusetts, USA, and the rest of the wood in the kitchen is also maple to maintain continuity. The dresser, which was in a different wood, was painted in the same green as the built-in cabinets – a delicate duck egg green from Martha Stewart's Arucana colours.

There are an enormous number of possessions to be stored in kitchens today, and, since this kitchen is also a dining room, Liz Shirley wanted to ensure that everything could be put away unobtrusively. She based her storage ideas on the walls of kitchen cabinets and doors that she had seen at Pleasant Hill Shaker Village, Kentucky, USA. Here an entire wall of drawers and cupboards housed the summer/winter clothes of the Shaker community, with each drawer carved to the exact size of the clothes to be stored, and filled with newly laundered clothes. By adapting the same practice of deciding exactly what she wanted to store under the stairs and measuring the cupboards and drawers to fit, she has managed to install a giant American fridge, a large drawer for pots and pans, a cutlery and table linens' drawer and a cupboard for vases and candlesticks. Using this method, she has kept most of the kitchen paraphernalia stored in one place. There are two more narrow cupboards for everything else, fitted either side of the Aga, each designed to look like another dresser pushed into the recess, although they are, in reality, fitted pieces of furniture.

LEFT: The Shaker kitchen is timeless and clean-lined enough to mix with almost any kind of china or cookware, but here the country feel is maintained with an old-fashioned kettle (TOP), rough earthenware bowls (CENTRE) and classic steel colander (BOTTOM). There is no pattern anywhere, just neutral or natural colours, and this helps pull the disparate elements together.

RIGHT: The Aga kitchen range with a Shaker peg rail overhead. The peg rail was a key element in Shaker design, as they used wall space for storage whenever they could. Here it is mainly decorative but is also used for kitchen implements. The heart symbol was used as a Shaker signature to denote piety; 'hands to work and hearts to God' was the credo of the community.

RIGHT: The area under the stairs has been maximized as storage space by copying the Shaker storage principles of making cupboards and drawers to fit each item exactly.

LEFT: A narrow fitted cupboard houses the boiler. The 'flyscreen' mesh allows air to escape.

LEFT: A Victorian pine dresser is painted duck egg green in order to avoid having too many different types of woods.

It is a key element in the Shaker look that each of these pieces of furniture is kept absolutely plain, with simple, round knobs and no beading or panelling. Although the Shakers did have decorative features, such as the heart or the Tree of Life, these were used very sparingly, as a kind of signature at the end of a piece of work rather than as a repeated pattern.

It is ironic that the Shakers actually scorned beauty. As Shaker Elder Frederick Evans of the Mount Lebanon community said: 'The beautiful...is absurd and abnormal. The divine man has no right to waste money upon what you call beauty in his house...while there are people living in misery.' Yet it was this very determination to strip away unnecessary frills and ornamentation, and their belief that good design was based on the function of the piece of furniture, that led to the making of beautiful, pared-down designs that have become forerunners of modern furniture today. The essence is extreme simplicity – beds did not have posters or tall bedposts, chairs used the minimum of wood that would make them functional, tables were made simply of legs and a top, and the only decoration was either a coat of paint or a wash that allowed the natural wood grain to show through. Otherwise wood was left natural. In this respect, their 200-year-old designs are as contemporary as anything made today. Their manufacturing techniques were also surprisingly modern. Shaker baskets, for example, were made close to factory-line methods, so that they could be made better and faster.

ABOVE: The key to these arrangements is
not to style them too carefully, and to
use just one or two kinds of flowers
rather than a wide variety. Add greenery
from your garden or a hedgerow.
Miniatures of Shaker-styled furniture
(CENTRE) can also make a charming
mantelpiece display, along with humble
spring flowers.

## BOXES AND BASKETS

THE SHAKERS WERE FAMOUS for having a place for everything and keeping everything
in its place, and they lived by the principle that everything you did, you should do as
well as you could to honour God. Shaker communities came mainly from northern
Europe, and emigrated from England, Sweden and other countries. They brought
together their native design traditions, then perfected and simplified them. The famous
oval Shaker boxes originated in Sweden, but it was the Shaker communities who added
swallow-tailed joins and used copper tacks to prevent rusting. The Shaker Shop has
taken the adaptation a step further, and has used the design for everything from small
boxes to bins for rubbish and linen.

The credo of the Shaker communities was 'beauty rests on utility' and although the
communities lasted less than 200 years in relatively small clusters on the north-east coast
of America, they have had a great impact on our lives through several inventions and
adaptations. The flat broom that is used around the world today, the apple corer and the
buzz saw were all Shaker inventions.

These designs are popular today, and can be mixed with other styles. Plan a Shaker
room, or just a Shaker peg rail. Where there are no Shaker equivalents – the style of flower
arrangements, for example – bring in the principles by using natural materials that have
been elegantly but simply arranged, carved or turned. The flowers, boxes and baskets
shown here all copy Shaker principles. Unpretentious spring flowers such as hyacinths, for
example, are displayed in a plain basket with garden greenery. This simple display shows
the Shaker ability to honour beauty from nature without making it over-elaborate.

RIGHT: Authentic copies of Shaker tables and chairs.

BELOW: Shaker boxes were adapted and improved by the Shaker communities from an old Swedish design, and now the adaptation continues to make the boxes work for 21st-century living. Shaker brooms (BOTTOM) re-shaped household brooms all over the world.

# NEW TRADITIONAL

LEFT: French country china (from Elizabeth Bauer in Bath, England), mixes eclectically with a check tablecloth and other hearty peasant pottery. The Hawaiian dancer in the background supplies a quirky note.

RIGHT AND ABOVE: Take your inspiration from the view outside your window. A colour scheme of lilac and soft blue was inspired by a lilac tree interwoven with clematis in the garden.

THE RE-USE, RE-CONDITIONING AND recycling of traditional materials to create a contemporary feel is at the heart of both this kitchen and From Somewhere, the knitwear design business of its owner Sasha de Stroumillo. With her partner Orsola de Castro, she re-works discarded knitwear, cutting up and re-stitching, patching or embroidering it into quirky, flattering designs, mixing the new and the old to create something unique. Here, a mass-market kitchen has been transformed into something that feels handmade and authentic by clever repainting and decorating techniques.

Faced with an outdated kitchen, many people would have started again, but this is not Sasha's philosophy. Theoretically a 'traditional' country kitchen, Sasha lightened and updated the look of the harsh 'orangey' pine cupboard fronts by removing their heavy relief panels and knobs, painting them creamy white and inserting holes instead of handles.

LEFT: Mixing classic rustic patterns, such as barleytwist china and check napkins (TOP) always works well. Cow parsley and anemones (CENTRE) echo the paint colours in the room. Sasha de Stroumillo collects and mixes bubble glass (BELOW) in different colours. A mixture of styles and colours work well together in glass for an informal, friendly look.

RIGHT: The kitchen table is the central work zone of the room, offering the main space for preparing and eating food, as well as being where the From Somewhere knitwear design business was started. The curtains were originally antique bedcovers bought from Faded Roses.

LEFT: Recycling is at the heart of this kitchen. By replacing the units' handles with holes, removing heavy relief panels and painting them white, a standard mass-market 'country' kitchen is given a facelift which makes it look custom-made. Adding a real wood work surface also makes the rest of the kitchen look much more authentic.

## COLOURS FROM THE GARDEN

THE KITCHEN'S COLOUR SCHEME is a contemporary take on traditional colours too. It was borrowed from the garden outside, where in spring a lilac tree blooms, entwined with the grey-green leaves and pinky-white flowers of a clematis. This combination of a soft, back-to-nature green, lilac and creamy white is the basis for the room, with the kitchen units painted white to make them lighter. The walls were painted lilac and the splashback tiles and inside of the cupboards green, which looks particularly attractive against white china and clear glass. It is by changing a few key elements of the room — for example, adding a quality maple work surface, instead of a cheap standard one, and changing the hob for a stylish stainless steel one — that make the most impact on the room — but at a very reasonable cost. The floor was made from cheap floorboards that were painted white — a practical, inexpensive way to make the room seem larger and lighter.

ABOVE: Plain china and clear glass storage jars (ABOVE LEFT) offer visual continuity and prevent clutter from looking like chaos. It's the small details that count — such as painting the inside of the cupboards green to match the tiles. When choosing fittings for taps (TOP), the simplest, cleanest lines will bridge the gap between classic and contemporary.

2 5

LEFT: The secret to relaxed style is never to take yourself too seriously – here fake flowers and shopping lists (FAR LEFT) hang haphazardly and the odd piece of kitsch – such as the Hawaiian dancer (BELOW) – enliven a collection of authentic antique china and glass.

## WELCOMING CLUTTER

NO COUNTRY KITCHEN, HOWEVER, is without some clutter. China evolves into mixed collections rather than being bought in formal sets. Mementoes, invitations, reminders of family life, flowers, candlesticks and diverse *objets trouvés* pile up in a friendly and welcoming way. While the design of the previous kitchen still gives the owners the opportunity to keep everything out of sight, but to hand when needed, the basis of this kitchen is to have it all on view, which is where the trusty dresser comes in. A dresser, either pine or painted, fitted or free-standing, is probably the key element that classifies a kitchen as 'country' – it is the ingredient that will not be found in a steel urban kitchen. Memories of the dresser are what most people recall about their country childhoods, and this one, which came from Robert Young Antiques, still has traces of its original Victorian paintwork. Piled high with well-loved collections, it stands as a piece of tradition among contemporary surroundings.

This is a kitchen where pattern and colour can sit comfortably together. The curtains were two old floral bedcovers, which turned out to be too long for the windows. However, the strip of fabric that had to be cut off came in useful to make ties to attach the curtains. The flowers have echoes of the lilac walls in their blooms, and the yellow of the curtains is repeated in the yellow blind.

In the summer, the big glass doors open up and the kitchen appears to be part of the garden, with soft natural colours inside melding with the real hues of nature outside. You could be in a rural paradise, but in fact a busy high street is situated only minutes away.

RIGHT: This antique pine dresser still has traces of its original Victorian paint. Leaving it intact, rather than renovating it to make it look smart, gives the room the feeling that it has always stood there. Don't make old furniture look too restored; the patina of age lends character to a room.

# SIMPLICITY

Reinterpret how traditional materials and patterns are used in a contemporary way to create a sense of freedom and an uncluttered lifestyle. Simplicity has always been at the heart of country style and features local materials, patterns and craftsmanship rather than elaborate furnishings.

# FLORALS

LEFT: Juxtapose a modern painting with a piece of traditional craftwork or an antique. The yellow in this abstract painting by Terry Frost is echoed in a few other yellow touches in the room, and also in this flower (RIGHT).

FLORALS ARE THE QUINTESSENTIAL country design. Colours and patterns are inspired by gardens and fields, many of which have become design classics. When combined with simple shapes and modern elements, old favourites gain a new dimension – the basic key is to use florals discreetly, or as decorative accents, in simple contemporary rooms to create a fresh, yet sophisticated, feel.

However, florals are wonderfully fresh, vivid and colourful, and work equally well in both contemporary and traditional schemes. And, of course, flowers are at the very heart of the countryside. There is nothing like a bunch of humble ranunculus casually placed in a jam jar, an innocent pot of primroses or a bouquet of fully blown garden roses to evoke the feeling that there is a luscious green garden, rolling woods and hedgerows situated just outside the door, rather than a busy one-way system and the smell of traffic fumes.

## CONTEMPORARY FLORALS

THIS ROOM IS A FORMAL town house drawing room, which many people might be tempted to decorate with 'important' furniture and expensive window treatments. However, the owners wanted to emphasize the feelings of light and space and they both have contemporary tastes. Gardening, in particular, is one of their passions so the idea of introducing a floral theme is very appropriate and draws the garden from the outdoors into the room. Although florals lost their reputation when they were married over-fussily to swags and frills and suffocated in scatter cushions, the key to a contemporary touch is to let them breathe. Simple, unfussy backgrounds such as plain cotton or linen upholstered sofas and chairs, white or simply painted walls and understated styling let the intrinsic charm of floral designs emerge in their own right.

The starting point for the room was an understated treatment based on white walls and modern High Street furniture from homestore chains such as Heals and Habitat in plain colours and natural fabrics. Such simplicity and discipline balance the wildness of the flowers: the chairs and sofa have a discreet scattering of floral cushions to add an accent, the white background to the fabric echoing the white of the walls. There is a creamy white jug of informal mixed flowers and a few neatly stitched flower-covered lavender bags on the mantelpiece, and, when tea is brought, floral plates with a white background make the perfect china. Nothing is overdone – the temptation to add floral china vases, floral rugs or chairs covered in floral fabrics has been avoided to keep the room as fresh and light as possible. The cushions haven't been matched – there are, in fact, several different designs in the room, but they are similar enough – all are rosy with spriggy flowers on a white background. Even the patterns are discreet and self-effacing: small-sprig florals are traditionally the decoration for cottages rather than castles, and were only used in grand houses as dust covers and linings.

RIGHT: Mix different floral patterns together for a relaxed, traditional look. The use of a white background on each keeps them fresh-looking and also pulls them together.

BELOW: Mix ages and styles: here contemporary high-street furniture looks good with collected pieces in a period house. The mantelpiece (LEFT) seems like stone, but was actually built from MDF (medium density fibreboard) by builders, then painted. The chair (CENTRE) features just one floral cushion as a striking accent. Contrast is also important in this light, contemporary style. Here an antique table and clock (RIGHT) sit happily with a modern painting and some expensive Shaker boxes.

## THE UNDERSTATED LOOK

WHITE IS A PARTICULARLY adaptable base to start with, but the same effect could be achieved with duck egg blue, soft misty or minty greens or neutral shades such as bone, ivory, beige or string. 'Historic' paint shades, or a cool, clear contemporary tint would make a good base colour for a floral room, but try to avoid featuring too many colours in the room to keep the look simple.

The palette of this room is essentially white, green and yellow, while only the odd dash of red in the rose pattern of the floral cushions adds that extra splash of colour. You could also achieve a similar effect by using the shades in any order you like – yellow walls with green or white chairs and sofas, or the green on the walls with yellow and white, and so on.

Colours that work well with florals include all the shades that are found in nature: from grass green to deepest moss; buttercup and daffodil yellows; hyacinth and forget-me-not blues; and the entire range of rose pinks, from the softest blush to a deep damson red. Your entire colour scheme could develop from picking out the shades in one scrap of favourite floral fabric, or from the flowers in your garden: lilac and green, for example, or blue and green. If you find that it starts to get too busy or the overall look seems too florid or overpowering, just introduce some neutral white or cream to calm the whole scheme down.

ABOVE: Simple shapes and neutral colours keep the look uncluttered: a Shaker sewing box, a creamy pottery jar and a simple Habitat vase with one flower in it (LEFT). Simple white china or clear glass makes an ideal foil for flowers of all kinds. Elaborate vases in a floral scheme would make it look too fussy (RIGHT).

ABOVE: A traditional tartan travelling rug, trimmed with velvet and updated by soft hues, blends in with the floral scheme (LEFT). Small spriggy floral colours always work well together (TOP).

LEFT: Details that count in floral decoration: beaded table mats and a napkin ring delicately made in the shape of a bee, a pretty blue embroidered bag (CENTRE) and a pile of soft luxurious suede notebooks in shades of rose, lilac and daffodil (BOTTOM).

RIGHT: A delicately stylized floral tablecloth. Different floral fabrics can work well together (FAR RIGHT). Calm Swiss embroidery is making a comeback (BOTTOM LEFT). The greens and pinks of the wallpaper are echoed in this vase of flowers (BOTTOM RIGHT).

## SIMPLICITY WITH FLORALS

FLOWERS AND FLORAL DESIGNS are amongst the world's best-loved patterns, but such popularity has also, on occasion, been their downfall. It is only a short step from a classic to a cliché, and, as a result, florals go through cycles in and out of fashion. However, florals are intrinsically fresh, vivid and colourful, so that they work equally well in contemporary and traditional schemes.

Florals suffered in popularity when they were treated in a way too fussy for their delicacy, cluttered up with trinkets or suffocated in pomp and scatter cushions. The key to a contemporary touch with flowers is to let them breathe. Simple backgrounds, such as plain cotton or linen upholstered sofas and chairs, white or simply painted walls and understated styling let the charm of floral designs emerge as stars in their own right.

Either traditional or modern patterns look good; just because you have contemporary tastes, there is no need to keep to stylized designs, when a spriggy Victorian print could look just as good. Different floral patterns work well together too, and you can also add other decorative textures, such as beading, embroidery, mirror mosaic or soft beautifully pastel shades of suede and silk, and finish it all off with a bunch of artlessly gathered real flowers.

# TEXTURES

RIGHT: The fragrance of incense stimulates the senses, enhancing the feeling of peace and serenity in the room. A shiny metallic electric fire (ABOVE) is an effective contrast to the natural wool and wood textures in the rest of the room.

LEFT: The walls are painted in a slightly grey-tinged mushroom white, which combines simplicity and sophistication. The fireplace is not used, but is kept opened up, so that it looks as if you could light a fire when you wanted. The roughness of the bricks and the original floorboards contrast with the sleek modern lines; when you are modernising, don't change everything.

THE USE OF TEXTURE rather than pattern is one of the ways that country elements can be used in sophisticated urban surroundings to introduce a feeling of serenity and calm. Decorating with texture is about appreciating the true nature of surfaces, rather than covering up or disguising them. This home belongs to stylist and furniture designer, Janie Jackson, who runs a decorative design company called Parma Lilac. The house is based in a smart part of town, but it is light and airy enough to be a home by the sea.

Extreme simplicity is the key to this look – bare boards and brick, white paint, and a few understated pieces of furniture. The lack of fussy detail means that even a relatively small room can be made to feel spacious, and there is a certain barefoot chic about it that is balm to the soul.

The colours in a textured room are usually neutrals and naturals, ranging from white and bone to the shades of pebbles and animal hide, and dark shades such as charcoal.

## DISCIPLINED STYLE

THE ORDERLY AND ALMOST monastic atmosphere of this sunny bedroom is maintained through rigorous discipline. In a crowded world where material possessions are prized and usually a priority, it can be liberating to be ruthless in editing what you wear and what you have around you, because it literally gives you space to think. The philosophy of making your life simpler by only buying or using possessions that you really do love or need is never going to be an easy one, and Janie Jackson admits to thinking very carefully before she buys anything and also to having regular, demanding clear-outs. However, they are worth it, for they give her the pleasure of waking up in a peaceful, airy, almost empty bedroom with sunlight streaming through the shutters.

The bed with its streamlined steel legs and base was designed by Janie Jackson for Parma Lilac, and is lighter and more airy-looking than the usual divan beds with their chunky bases. It sits relatively high; there is space underneath for storing boxes and baskets, or it could be left as a clutter-free space.

Simple white cotton or linen bedding is the only option for such a calm environment, and the addition of a textured wool blanket from Wales adds an element of interest to the smooth surfaces of steel and white paint.

The shutters are particularly clever, as they are made of Perspex and designed by Janie Jackson to offer a practical, contemporary alternative to net curtains. They are completely opaque, but let in light and are less heavy and obvious than wooden shutters.

There is no art or ornament required in a room like this; some pebbles from a beach or smooth black stones are all that is required to remind you of the beauty of nature.

ABOVE AND LEFT: Texture is at its most satisfying in traditional materials: wool, wood, steel and glass, like those contained in this vase and bedcover. They have a depth about them that is lacking in plastics. Mix round and smooth textures, and look for natural objects, such as alliums, that have architectural shapes in order to achieve the feel of a timeless but contemporary summer house situated in the woods.

ABOVE: Paint a naturally dark room yellow to maximize a feeling of light (ABOVE RIGHT). Open shelving looks more spacious than cupboards, and these linens become part of the overall decoration of the room. This is a stylish new idea for storing bedding and towels.

## STORAGE AND DECORATION

THIS BEDROOM AND DRESSING ROOM were originally two rooms, but Janie Jackson knocked down the wall between them to open up the space. The front of the house, where the bedroom is, was light and painted white, but the dressing room faced north, so she painted it yellow for warmth. The theme of transparency and freedom from clutter is maintained by having open shelves and a plain hanging rail in place of wardrobes. Open floorspace was retained by building shelves on either side of the windows.

The floors were also painted off-white to maximize the light, and their slightly shiny surfaces reflect the sun too. With just one table and mirror to complete the set-up, the whole room is a pared-down and feminised version of the traditional country house men's dressing room. No decoration is needed, because the clothes with their textures of cotton, silk and wool, are on full view. Their soft colours range from calm neutrals to pastels.

43

LEFT: Venetian mirrors – where a mirror frame surrounds a central mirror – were fashionable in the 18th and 19th centuries. In a plain, simple room, one outrageous or elaborate item adds impact and character. The lightness achieved by having mirror surrounded by mirror offers a contrast of texture which does not overwhelm. Sitting on a neat table, it also makes an ideal dressing table (BELOW).

RIGHT: The carefully planned shelves and open hanging rail were designed by Janie Jackson for her company Parma Lilac. This look requires discipline but saves time hunting for clothes in the morning.

## TEXTURE IN THE BATHROOM

DECORATING WITH TEXTURE CAN also mean taking one texture and working with variations of it. Here the glassy nature of water reflects the essentially shiny mix of textures for a bathing area. Steel, tin, china, glass and painted wood harmonize together rather than contrasting each other. There is nothing unnecessary in the room: semi-circular stools, also designed by Janie Jackson for Parma Lilac, are calm and simple, a single tap combines hot and cold water, and the plumbing of the square china basin is left exposed. Opaque glass is used at the windows, so no curtains are needed, allowing the elegant lines of the sash window to be enjoyed.

Bathrooms in the country are often thought of as bleak, chilly outposts – while the ones situated in towns and cities tend to be associated with luxury and pampering. Yet in today's centrally heated homes, a bare, simple bathroom can be like a breath of fresh, country air. In a built-up area where there are many houses, some elaborately furnished, it is a new indulgence to be restrained and plain.

## PRACTICAL CONSIDERATIONS

THERE ARE PRACTICAL ASPECTS to simplicity – notably the plumbing. Here the drain of the basin is on full view, but the plumbing behind the single tap has been concealed. and the piping has been chased into brickwork and covered up with plaster – but it's worth checking with your local plumber and finding out whether the tap washers will get furred up quickly. You don't want to re-decorate every time you change a washer.

BELOW: As well as contrasting textures, you can also unify them: here, steel, china and glass echo the shiny surface of water. Use dual-purpose furniture to keep the look simple: semi-circular stools are also used to hold towels and bathroom accessories, while a painted table holds a large mirror.

RIGHT: Simplicity means honesty: that is why the metallic waste pipe has been left on view in this minimalist bathroom.

# Decorating with
# COLOUR & PATTERN

COLLECTIONS OF PATTERNS, COLOUR, AND CLASSIC PATTERNS LIKE FLORALS AND CHECKS USED IN FRESH CONTEMPORARY WAYS ARE THE SUBSTANCE OF THIS STYLE. YOU CAN ALSO EMULATE A STUNNING, ECLECTIC ATMOSPHERE THAT BORROWS FROM THE GREAT ENGLISH COUNTRY HOUSES OF THE PAST AND GIVES THEM A MODERN TWIST.

# FADED PATTERNS

RIGHT AND LEFT: These wooden kitchen units were custom built to the owner's sketches by carpenters, which can be a surprisingly cost-effective way of getting a kitchen made to your own personal specifications.

THE QUINTESSENTIAL LOOK OF English country house style is a relaxed mix of colour and pattern, often faded with wear and eclectic in the way it's put together. This is probably the world's most welcoming and natural style of decorating, which evolves over the years, and is never quite 'finished'. It is an organic way of living, which looks pretty but is also primarily practical, and this house, home of the stylist Lucinda Chambers at British Vogue, exemplifies this kind of English style in its most contemporary form.

Floral patterns, such as chintzes, damasks and toiles, along with classic stripes, checks and textured plains, plus collections – anything from plates to handbags – are at the heart of this unusual, but comfortable look. Everything looks used, because it is used, although many shops now stock fabrics that are made to look 'faded' or tea-stained with age in order to re-create a sense of timelessness.

ABOVE: The key to the faded style is that nothing matches: wicker and wooden chairs sit together (LEFT), different classic patterns of Cornish blue-and-white and Denby pottery are combined with more delicate rose-tinted plates (CENTRE), and the plates themselves are all bought at random in twos and threes, or singly, from flea markets and second-hand shops (RIGHT).

## A THEME OF ROSES

HERE THE KITCHEN IS a glorious home for Lucinda's collection of china, and fabric with roses on it. Old roses and new ones, bright and faded roses, roses from the East and from the West, rosy fabrics, plates, mugs and rosy hues and tints of every kind mingle together in a glorious symphony. Nothing is contrived or arranged, so family and guests feel free to linger and lounge, without worrying about disarranging a carefully thought-out scheme. It's a real home, not a photographic image which will be spoilt when someone throws a school bag or a pile of shopping on the table. It is a home with a heart and soul, not a reflection of fashion.

Although this style seems to have no limits at all, the collections do offer a unifying theme for those who don't know where to start with such a rambling look. Here it is roses, but other themes could be florals in general, shades and patterns in blues, small patterns, checks and stripes, or even a scheme inspired by the colours and patterns of a teapot collection or Thirties china. The pleasure of such a theme is that china, glass, fabrics and furniture don't have to be expensive; many of these plates were found in junk shops, and if someone breaks one, Lucinda throws it away and happily replaces it.

The next element of this style is that nothing matches. The dining room chairs are plain wooden kitchen chairs, but in different styles. The detail on the built-in kitchen units varies on each side of the room. On one side, tongue-and-groove boarding is set into a frame, with small inset silver handles. On the other side, the detailing is plainer, with old-fashioned steel drawer handles. Both sides are painted white – although they could easily have been painted different colours – and all have steel handles, but that is all that matches.

RIGHT: Mismatched chairs around the kitchen table create a relaxed atmosphere, reflected in an informal bunch of blue and pink flowers in a humble jug. As well as mixing old and new, and different styles, this look juxtaposes the grand and the humble: the fireplace is marble and is usually found in a more formal-looking room. However, here it has an air of faded grandeur.

BELOW: This style is ideal for magpies; anything pretty can be displayed, such as this charming painted wooden egg.

## CUSTOM-MADE KITCHENS

THIS KITCHEN WAS DESIGNED by Lucinda Chambers herself. She sketched out what she wanted for the builder to copy. If you can't find what you like in the brochures of kitchen companies, or if you have a house in a distinctive style you'd like to mirror, don't be afraid of commissioning your own kitchen units and having them built by craftsmen or carpenters. This can be a surprisingly cost-effective option, but think about what you need and how you use the kitchen before having everything built.

This look could be described as organic because it grows with the house, but it must also be practical. The table settles where it is most convenient. An old sofa or chair is placed where people like to sit. The cupboard that contains the vacuum cleaner or brushes is kept in the most convenient place, not where a designer has deemed it should go. While your impulse is often to get a house 'straight' as soon as you move into it, you often create a more natural feeling if you live somewhere for several months before deciding what you want where. See where the light falls at different times of day, what the best views are with the seasons, and where people like to congregate.

Many of the patterns and styles are classic – if they're not genuinely old, they're patterns that have been in use for a hundred years or more, and are often still made by the same company. Every country has its own version of striped blue-and-white Cornish creamware, Denby pottery, enamel breadbins, classic electric toasters and English chintzes; put all of these styles together to create a house that looks as if it has been lived in for generations.

RIGHT: The mantelpiece arrangement is not contrived: like everything else in the house, it has grown organically as more pretty treasures are brought home. Valuable items, like silver candlesticks, can sit next to flea market finds and smooth stones found on country walks.

BELOW: There is a theme of roses in these rooms, and they can be found on literally every surface from china to fabric (LEFT). Open shelving and a plate rack help to display everything (RIGHT).

# BLUE/WHITE KITCHEN

ABOVE: Blue flowers in white vases echo the theme of the kitchen.

LEFT: This is another 'recycled' kitchen. Here a continuous run of brown Seventies units were painted white. Good tricks to copy include: taking a few units out and replacing them with a plate rack or basket drawers to break up the run, making it look more modern and less ordered. Add a white fretwork strip at the bottom of the shelves as a pretty decorative effect.

BLUE AND WHITE is a classic colour combination, but it's friendly and relaxed, evoking memories of country dairies, seaside deck chairs and Cornish china. Almost every country in the world has a tradition of using blue and white in kitchens and in cookware, from English striped tea towels and Dutch Delft tiles to the glorious slatey blues of the paintwork in French farmhouse kitchens or the blue-and-white French enamel kitchenware that is now considered so collectable. The combination of blue and white is fresh, pretty and contemporary, without being folksy. Most importantly it's an effect that looks equally good with any budget, and can be very flexible. This kitchen here, for example, is predominantly white, with the blue featuring in the table linen and china, which means that the emphasis can easily be altered if tastes or fashions change.

The starting point for this kitchen was economy. Replacing a kitchen is often one of the biggest investments made in a house and, when you've just moved in, it's

ABOVE: Stripes and checks
are classic patterns for a
blue-and-white theme, and
create a light, fresh
atmosphere.

LEFT: A small bunch of anemones or
ranunculus placed casually in a plain blue
glass vase adds a light, informal touch to
the kitchen. There's no need to worry
about balance or arrangement – the
effect that is created is similar to a
wildflower arrangement with blooms
that have been picked by a child on
a country walk.

often best to see what you can do with the kitchen that's there before spending a large sum on a new one. Faced with an outdated brown fitted L-shaped kitchen, the owner, Suzanne Sharp of The Rug Company, instantly made it feel lighter and more modern by painting the units white. She believes that painting something white to brighten it up, and then living with it for a while, is often the best way to proceed.

## CHANGING THE DESIGN

MANY PEOPLE CHANGE the doors on a fitted kitchen to alter the design, but you can create a different look even more effectively – and cheaply – by remodelling one or two elements. For example, this kitchen had been a continuous L-shape of base and wall units. She removed two wall units to break the run and open out the space, making it feel more organic and relaxed. This gave the feeling that the scheme had evolved rather than being designed. She also took off some doors – not all – to create some open shelves, and added a wall-hung plate rack. While all the doors on the lower units were retained but painted white, two doors on the upper units were replaced with wooden ones, with the planks laid laterally. The changes made were very small, but they freed up the rigid, outdated design very effectively.

Finally, she added a fretwork strip from the British mail order company, Jali, along the bottom of the units. It softens the hard lines of the modern units and is reminiscent of old-fashioned shelves with cotton, embroidered shelf liners.

ABOVE: Food covers (LEFT) were used in old-fashioned kitchens to protect food from being attacked by flies. Now they're making a comeback because so much produce – such as fruit or cheese – tastes better if it's not kept in the fridge. Everyday, inexpensive tumblers (CENTRE) are just right to add to the informal effect. Collectable blue and white fine china (RIGHT) can also easily be mixed with budget chain-store purchases to great effect.

ABOVE: These shelves were originally a fitted cupboard but the doors were removed and fretwork added to change the look of it without spending huge amounts of money (LEFT). Open shelves tend to be best for kitchenware that is used every day, so that items do not become dusty or pick up kitchen grime. The plate rack (RIGHT) provides both a storage area and a place for plates to dry, thus bypassing the time-consuming 'putting away' ritual.

Mixing closed cupboards with open shelves is an effective way of making a design look more relaxed. The most convenient kitchenware to display on open shelves are those used every day, such as plates and glasses. The one disadvantage of open shelving is that items can get sticky or dusty from the kitchen's atmosphere, but if everything is being constantly used, that is not a problem. Open shelves also mean that china and glass become integrated into the decorative scheme.

Keeping to a theme, such as blue, blue-and-white, or white china emphasizes the look, and prevents it from becoming too cluttered and untidy. Odd plates and cups can sit together very attractively, and expensive china can be mixed with cheaper buys to achieve harmony. It also offers scope for storing collections. You can go as far as you like by adding blue-and-white tablecloths and napkins, bowls, jugs, vases and flowers. Blue and white fabrics can be found in any style, from a traditional Fifties design like this tablecloth by Cath Kidston, to cheerful farmhouse stripes and checks and vibrantly modern designs.

Flooring is often considered a major issue in kitchens, because of spilt food and heavy traffic. This often encourages many people to choose dark colours in the belief that they will need less cleaning. However, light floors keep the decorative emphasis where it should be, on the furnishings and decorations of the room, and also make limited spaces appear bigger. Here the floorboards were simply sanded down and painted white, and they have already survived several years of family life before needing re-painting.

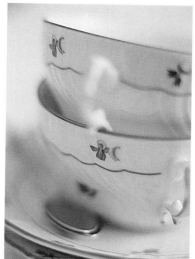

ABOVE: The delicate floral pattern of this china and glassware fits into the blue and white theme well.

RIGHT: A bunch of scented spring narcissi blends in well with the colour scheme and also adds a wonderful fragrance to the kitchen.

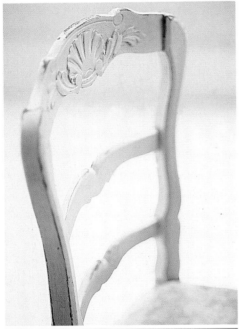

LEFT: Transform heavy items with white paint: an iron chandelier has been painted white, with little glass droplets simply tied on, making it an interesting focal point in the room. Old wooden chairs have been painted a distressed white (CENTRE) to give them a friendly freshness reminiscent of Swedish style. China, glass and cutlery (BOTTOM) have been carefully chosen to maintain the blue-and-white theme.

RIGHT: One single over-sized item in a small room often can make it seem bigger and grander than it really is. Here the chandelier fulfils that function well. A comfortable armchair (INSET) in a spriggy floral fabric helps to bring a note of comfort to the room.

## ELEGANT DINING

THIS GLORIOUSLY LIGHT and refined dining area is adjacent to the blue and white kitchen, and follows its decorative theme in a way that is both understated and grand. The room itself is square with floor-to-ceiling windows. It is not particularly large, but it does, however, have a high ceiling. One of the top interior decorator tricks used to make a small area seem grander and larger than it is, is to have one extra-large out-of-scale focal point that makes a stunning single statement. Here the room's main asset, the high ceiling, is utilized, and the focal statement is a large iron candelabra, again painted white by Suzanne Sharp. It would have been just as dramatic to leave it as its original ironwork, but painting it white makes it lighter and more delicate, and just as outrageous, but not as overbearing. She also added droplets of coloured glass in blue and red to emphasize its decorative effect.

A big country kitchen table and some French-looking ladderback chairs, also painted white, along with an old armchair in a faded floral fabric, complete the effect. With the white painted walls and floor, the room needs no more decoration. Including any paintings or ornaments would distract from the sweeping spaciousness that has been evoked by the elements of Swedish influence.

Swedish style has had a great deal of influence on today's contemporary interiors, because it is light and modern, yet very decorative. To encapsulate the look, keep windows bare or use simple transparent muslin drapes (light is important in a northern country), have white, grey or pastel walls, use candles (on long, dark Swedish nights they increase the sense of light), and use wooden furniture, as it is a country covered in pine forests.

# SEASIDE HUES

ABOVE: Displaying beach mementoes such as this starfish, or framing simple objects (RIGHT), is an effective way of displaying collections.

LEFT: Seaside fabrics, such as checks and florals, are bright, cheerful and honest and work well together when the scale of the patterns is similar. The furniture included here shows how different styles can look good together when they are uniformly painted white.

THE SEA AND ITS ASSOCIATED COUNTRYSIDE hold evocative memories for most people of long, hot summer holidays. It is a perfect inspiration for decorating, particularly for children's rooms and bathrooms. These children's rooms, designed by Suzanne and Christopher Sharp of the British-based Rug Company, have all the naïve charm of a holiday, ranging from the traditional bucket-and-spade holiday of British beaches to the carnival atmosphere and palm-fringed exotica of the tropics.

When taking such a theme as inspiration for decorating, always look at the colour elements first. The ingredients of the coast are the colours of the sea and sand – blue and cream – along with brighter colours, such as reds and candy pinks, that look so effective under an open sky. All these colours are punctuated with plenty of white. Then identify typical patterns: seaside fabrics are bright and honest, such as checks and stripes, and the proximity of sun and wind means they can look just that little bit worn and faded.

LEFT: These elaborate beds were found second-hand in a junk shop. They were obviously brought over from India by a local family, and discarded when the children outgrew them. They were originally dark teak, but have taken on a completely different look when painted white. Cushions (CENTRE) can be trimmed with ribbon and a curtain (BOTTOM) made to look more modern by adding a contrasting hem. The ribbon above and the row of bobbles helps to disguise the fact that they were later additions.

RIGHT: Always try several shades of paint in large panels on several walls before deciding on exactly the right tone of colour for a room. A room's natural light changes the way the colour appears. This Blue Moon, from the Fired Earth company, looks calm and neutral, evoking the essence of the sea in the northern light of this bedroom, but would appear to be almost a turquoise shade in a south-facing room.

There will also always be a few building techniques or fittings, such as tongue-and-groove boarding, or certain styles of flooring, that can be adapted. Here, boarding has been used on a central landing, from which all the children's rooms open. A narrow shelf at chest height, resembling a dado rail, displays a range of seaside souvenirs – such as framed holiday photographs and sailing boats. These set the tone for the rooms leading off it.

## HOW TO CHOOSE COLOUR

A HALL IS A UNIFYING AREA, and needs to lead smoothly into the rooms off it, so even if they are very different colours some element should unite them. Colour themes are the ideal way of providing this. Here, plenty of white, painted on the furniture and walls, prevents the different colours from appearing too busy and links them together.

Another important consideration when choosing colour is how much natural light each room receives. Here, two rooms face north, while the third faces south, and can take bright colours well. The north-facing rooms are the hardest to choose colours for, because bright colours can seem too strong, and paler ones too dull. Blues can be particularly changeable: the blue bedroom, for example, is painted in Blue Moon, a shade from the Fired Earth company. It is delicately neutral in a north-facing room, but becomes almost turquoise in a Southerly room. It is, therefore, vitally important to paint sample panels of paint on the walls, as Suzanne Sharp did – taking weeks, or even months – before deciding which shade you think will achieve the desired effect. Choosing a paint from swatches on card just does not give a true impression of what it will look like on the wall.

ABOVE: A great child's room is a mix of the practical and funky: here a simple, white table from a home-store chain such as IKEA makes a useful desk (RIGHT). Quirky objects such as this zebra stool (CENTRE) look good in this brightly coloured room. To achieve a relaxed, yet coherent effect with pattern, make sure that the colours used are similar as shown here with this attractive jumble of bedlinen (LEFT).

OPPOSITE: The holiday theme is picked up in this room's carnival colours. As it is south-facing, it can take stronger colours, such as this vivid pink. A good trick is to paint half the wall white, as seen here, to make the colour look fresher and less dominating. Colours of a similar brightness look good together.

## FINDING INSPIRATION

Deciding on a theme and making it work in a room means experimenting with what
works and what doesn't, but it's worth risking a few mistakes to have a home that you
really enjoy rather than one which feels 'safe' and ordinary. You can take inspiration
from your garden (see *New Traditional* kitchen on pages 20–29), from a bunch of
flowers seen in a florist's window, from the combination of shells, sand, seawater and a
blue, blue sky on the beach, or from something more immediately corresponding to a
home, such as the pages of a magazine or book, or a shop window.

Look at the elements: the colours, the objects and the patterns and begin to set up
a swatchboard. This is an interior designer trick: you take small pieces of paint or
fabric, and pin them together on a board to see how they work. Then switch them
around to see how the balance of colour and atmosphere changes. Once you have a

RIGHT: Having shelves at shoulder height is a good way of displaying items like this authentic Victorian dolls' house. It also protects it as it is too precious for children to play with unsupervised. A model lighthouse, such as this one (BOTTOM), is a good seaside link and can be bought in coastal towns everywhere.

scheme you like, however, you must try it out over as large an area as possible. This doesn't just mean the paint – fabric and flooring are just as important. Many shops will sell large sample swatches of fabric, and return the fee if you return the swatch (this is useful if you're going to buy expensive fabric). If the fabric is affordable, buy a metre of it and drape it over furniture for a few days to see how it works. If you don't want to paint panels of paint in your room, buy plain lining wallpaper, paint that and pin it up. Reputable rug companies will also lend rugs for a few days so that you see them in situ. Place the chair or sofa you're hoping to re-cover (or a similar one) draped in the fabric swatch, and live with the large-scale re-creation of your swatchboard in one corner until you've decided it's right for the whole room.

## THE FINAL TOUCHES

These add the character to a room: the lighthouse, the doll's house, the little beach huts... If your budget is tight, try looking in junk shops for pieces that are a little bit different and can be transformed with fabric, wallpaper or paint. As their intrinsic value is not great, you can afford to experiment and, if they become damaged by bathroom use, you can always throw them out. For these rooms, a kitchen chair and an Indian mirror add character to decor at a very low cost. The chair could be found almost anywhere, but it has been painted white and given a new seat in a vivid fabric. A chair like this gives you a real chance to have fun. It could be painted in bright colours or given an antique look with historic colours and a distressed finish. It could even be made to seem ultra-luxurious by adding a small square of a very expensive fabric to the seat. So, if there's a piece of fabric you've fallen in love with but can't afford, this is a great way to add it to your decorative scheme. Not only are these ideas inexpensive, but they can all be done in an afternoon.

The key to successful shopping from second-hand shops is to go in every time you pass one. Piled in amongst the unattractive items of poor quality, there may be one or two that are worth buying, but you need to go and look regularly to find them. If Suzanne Sharp sees something she likes, she buys it, regardless of whether she really needs it, because she knows that she will never find exactly the same thing in a junk shop again.

ABOVE: Tongue-and-groove boarding and a peg rail create a seaside/country feel. A display cabinet can be used to hold holiday treasures.

BELOW: A wire basket makes a useful container for bathroom nick-nacks or *objet trouvés*.

## THE BATHROOM

A BATHROOM CAN BE the ultimate fantasy room. It is usually small enough to make buying expensive paint or paper affordable, and it can be re-decorated quickly if you tire of the theme. It is a room to relax in – a place where you can be whisked away mentally to another world. But is not a room where you linger as long as in kitchens, living rooms and bedrooms, so there is less chance of getting bored with the decoration.

A nautical or seaside fantasy is one of the most attractive themes for bathrooms, and can be easy to achieve, even with mass-market fittings and in a tiny space. This bathroom was created on a strict budget, with all the fixtures, fittings and tongue-and-groove boarding coming from a DIY chain, and basic pine shelving from home store IKEA.

Once you have bought the basics – a white bathroom suite, shelving, towel rails and somewhere to keep bathroom paraphernalia, you can let your imagination fly. Some interior decorators believe that colour is the last thing to add. So get the bathroom layout and fittings right, and choose the room's colour.

## CHOOSING A COLOUR

ALTHOUGH YOU CAN USE WALLPAPER in a bathroom – the steam is less damaging than you might expect and you'll certainly get a good few years of wear out of it – paint is usually a better option. If you've inherited a bathroom that you don't like, try painting it to lift the atmosphere before replacing it altogether. However, it is difficult to paint tiles well, and it can look a bit cheapskate. If you can't afford to re-tile, cover it up inexpensively, with plyboard or tongue-and-groove. However, if this is regularly splashed, such as behind a shower, it will need re-painting more often, although today's acrylic paints are fairly water-resistant. Here, paint has been used to make cheap pine look timeless and chic.

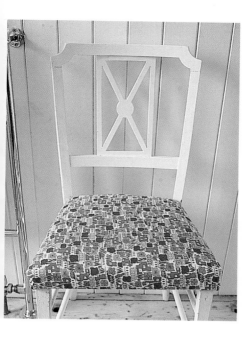

ABOVE: A junk-shop chair can be transformed by using a fun fabric on the seat.

RIGHT: A shelf above tongue-and-groove boarding in the bathroom offers another opportunity to show themed items, as well as being a useful place for shampoo bottles and other bathroom paraphernalia. A display case – this is a second-hand shopfitting – is a good way of displaying, but also protecting, favoured items in a bathroom.

# Natural
# ELEMENTS

The grain of real wood is a starting point for two very different approaches: the calm, clean, puritanical designs evoked by New England and a mellow approach to modern design in a room that happily mixes wood with man-made materials.

# NEW ENGLAND

LEFT AND ABOVE: A simple trestle table and Wishbone chairs are the only furniture in the dining end of this double room. The brick surroundings and the wood of the log fire look almost like a work of art against the white walls.

THE SNOWY VASTNESSES OF New England, the mountains and pine trees, the four-month winters, and the simplicity of the clapboard houses, is evoked here in a contemporary white-and-wood room in a town basement. The clarity of the mountain air, the sense of space, and the grainy, satisfying texture of wood are the inspiration, letting you believe that you are in a mountain hideaway in the woods, rather than in a busy city. When the first American settlers arrived on the East Coast, they brought the house-building skills and tastes of northern Europe with them, but both new architectural and interior styles soon evolved. The tough life, lack of time, and raw materials – except for wood – meant that initially houses were simple and box-like. They were made of clapboard (this term refers to the noise of board hitting board as the house was built) with little detailing, either inside or out. This simplicity has now become synonymous with chic modern style, yet still evokes a time when life was based on honest, country occupations.

LEFT: Complement a simple, understated decor with elegant pottery in neutral and natural colours.

ABOVE: An old wooden trestle against white-painted tongue-and-groove creates a rustic yet airy effect.

RIGHT: Washable loose covers are practical and stylish on white armchairs, and the effect of white on white makes the room seem bigger and lighter than it is.

## PRACTICAL STYLE

THE WHITE-PAINTED bare boards and walls are the starting point for this look and the rest of the room is very disciplined and restrained. Even though the effect of white on white makes the room seem bigger and ligher than it really is, it could almost be called stark, except for the warmth and smoothness of the wooden chairs. They are modern designs known as Wishbone Chairs, but were purchased in an antique market. Many pieces of modern furniture have become design classics, and purchasing them second-hand is a good way of acquiring them at a reasonable price. There is an added attraction to them in that wood acquires a friendly patina when it is used and worn; chairs straight from the factory would not have quite the same depth of tone as these. The dining table is a simple trestle design, in keeping with the clean lines and rustic nature of the overall theme.

LEFT: The space under the stairs is used for storage, but is left open in order to increase the sense of light and space.

BELOW: In a disciplined, pared-down environment, a few colourful decorative touches such as these pretty lanterns and coloured glass doorknobs (BOTTOM) add that special sparkle.

## NATURAL SHADES

WASHABLE LOOSE COVERS in white are a practical, yet stylish, way of covering armchairs, which may be placed around a log fire. Anyone who has ever been to the New England states – Vermont, Maine or Massachusetts – will be aware of the importance of log fires and log stoves. With the abundance of trees, and winter temperatures which often go down to 35 degrees below zero, the log fire or stove is the symbol of winter warmth and protection.

Simple pottery or china in neutral or natural shades, or white, fits best with this look, and there are no pictures or ornaments. During the early days of the Settlers in America, fine china and porcelain – if people could afford it – was supplied and imported by English factories, but America soon became self-sufficient in thick cream or white-coloured china, often known as creamware or stoneware. Huge stoneware jars were found in every household to store pickled vegetables, home-made beer, oils – in fact anything that needed to be kept over the winter. Chunky white or cream plates and mugs are an intrinsic part of American style today; the influence of the early settlers can still be detected in the thick mugs and plates that are used in diners and cafés everywhere in America in the 21st century.

These items – bare wood, plain walls, white or neutral china, log fires and lack of ornamentation – create a very contemporary look, but it's worth stopping to reflect that it was a style created by hardship. Life, in the midst of incredible natural beauty, was tough in New England for everyone except the very rich until the middle of the last century.

# URBAN COUNTRY

RIGHT: These storage jars have a sleek ceramic finish which is combined with more traditional styling. Displaying them on an open shelf is very much the country kitchen style.

LEFT: The juxtaposition of the natural and the purely man-made is shown here. Formica worktops with wood edging and steel uprights create a contemporary and practical look.

THIS IS THE MOST CONTEMPORARY of the country kitchens, and shows how you can adapt just one or two significant elements of a look for 21$^{st}$-century living. This large, light kitchen is in a basement of a town house, and the owner, stylist Liz Bauwens, wanted a friendly country kitchen with a contemporary feel. A relaxing atmosphere and room enough for children to run in and out from the garden were her main criteria. City kitchens today can be similar in style to steel operating theatres – slick and smart – but country kitchens too often become associated with clutter. This kitchen takes three elements from a country kitchen – an Aga cooking range, the use of real wood for some of the furniture and trims and the idea of creating as much space as possible. These were then made to work organically with the architecture of the house.

Many of the design principles – a few fitted units, a mix of china and glass, and many displayed items – evoke a country kitchen, but how they are put together is very modern.

LEFT: Here contemporary design has been combined with traditional materials: wooden chairs by designer Arne Jacobsen and a marine ply table with a Formica 'surfboard' top which is supported by steel legs.

RIGHT: The white Aga kitchen range is the focal point of the room. The alcoves on either side have deliberately been left empty to create an airy feel. The wall by the window is a false wall, and conceals steel security grilles which can be drawn shut over the French windows for protection when the house is empty.

## THE STARTING POINT

THE AGA, A SYMBOL OF TRADITION, was the starting point. However, in white, in a white room, it looks completely modern – clean and stylish. It's an enormous cooking range, making a big focal statement in the room, so Liz Bauwens decided to leave its surroundings as airy as possible. In the alcoves on either side of the chimney, there is a low table and chest, instead of the ceiling-length cupboards that might otherwise have been installed. This allows the architecture of the room to be on display. The high shelf for pans, and a long rail for hanging kitchen implements, have been fitted discreetly, without altering the proportions of the room. If you have any interesting features in your room, perhaps a chimney, a big window, an alcove or just an oddly shaped room, it gives the scheme more warmth and character to show them off, rather than covering them up with a standard run of units.

Because of the width of the room, a central island, designed by British furniture maker David Coote, was a good option. The debate on whether or not to have a central island is important in the design of any kitchen today. Incorporating one adds a friendly work

LEFT: If you take a theme for china, such as white, blue-and-white, or floral, you can mix the patterns and styles together without creating a cluttered, untidy look.

LEFT: In the living part of the kitchen, a miniature table and chairs has been included for the children. A new take on flowers – this big floral design has been painted in a stylised fashion on one of the cupboard fronts (BELOW).

RIGHT: White china and clear glass are displayed on open shelves for a clean, streamlined appearance. The ingredients of this kitchen design, such as natural wood and a marble top for food preparation, are timeless, but the clean styling of this chest (FAR RIGHT) makes it entirely contemporary.

RIGHT: Use a central island to divide the kitchen into specific work areas: the dishwasher faces china and glass storage cupboards and a double sink unit is conveniently close to the cookers. An inexpensive chest, with simple pull-out drawers (FAR RIGHT), has been included to hold small items. It can also be painted to suit different colour schemes.

OPPOSITE: Some shapes, such as the jug of cooking utensils (LEFT) and the coffee pot (RIGHT), are more traditional in style, but others, such as the tap (CENTRE), are strictly modern, yet they all work well together.

BELOW: Make the most of a room's natural architecture by using free-standing chests or tables rather than full-length cupboards, as this keeps the atmosphere as airy and light as possible. Here, pots, cooking implements and ingredients – along with contemporary photography – are all on display, almost farmhouse style.

area that faces the room. It is also a good way of breaking up a large room, but is not space effective in a smaller room. And, unlike a central table, it cannot be moved and so is relatively inflexible. This central island features a sink, waste-disposal unit, and a beech work surface for food preparation, which makes the journey from the cooker to the sink short and easy. It is also means that, with small children around, it is safer, because food preparation and cooking are then limited to one small area in a large room – another good trick for making living in a large kitchen less demanding.

## CLEVER PLANNING

A CENTRAL ISLAND can help kitchen planning enormously by placing working areas close to each other. Here the dishwasher opens facing the other side of the kitchen where the only kitchen storage units are, which house all the china and glass. So when the dishwasher is used, the cutlery, glass and china can be unloaded directly from it into the storage cupboards – another labour-saving trick for a large kitchen.

Once again, the white surface is modern, but it has a natural wooden edging to soften the look. Some china and glass kitchenware is kept behind closed doors, while some is out on display. This is another way of making a modern kitchen look relaxed and appear more friendly.

Having organized the work areas of the kitchen, the eating and play areas were next. The essential strength of farmhouse kitchens is that they are places where everything happens. They are often the warmest place in winter – the central point where everyone

gathers to discuss and plan the day as well as eat, and, of course a place for young children to play. One important point to bear in mind when planning a kitchen is to recognize the importance of keeping living, working and playing zones clearly demarcated, as hot pans do not mix well with a children's playing area. Keeping activities confined to one part of a room also makes the room easier to tidy: children's books and toys can be kept near where they are used, and so on.

## A MODERN AND CLASSIC COMBINATION

A KITCHEN WITH BOTH modern and traditional design elements can have any kind of a kitchen table. A classic pine kitchen table can accentuate the traditional theme, whereas this table's design, based on a surfboard with its slightly rounded edges, emphasizes the contemporary look, as do the chairs from the well-known modernist designer Arne Jacobsen. To keep the look uncluttered, all the storage jars and china are either white, steel or glass. But there is a friendly assortment of different styles and makes, as if they had all been collected organically over the years rather than having been bought together in one coordinated shopping trip.

Concealing the less attractive aspects of today's world, such as crime prevention measures, also makes the kitchen seem more timeless. Here, the French windows at the back needed security grilles to keep out unwanted intruders. To conceal these when they are open, Liz Bauwens had a fake 'panelled' wall built in front of them, which was painted white like the rest of the room. When they are closed, they just slide away between the real wall and the fake panelling, and are completely hidden.

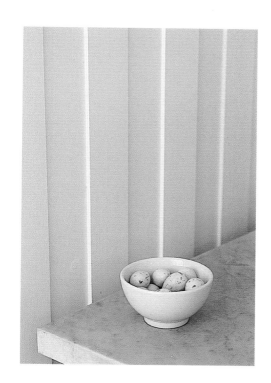

ABOVE: The panelled wall behind this bowl is false, cleverly concealing the less appealing, but necessary, security grilles.

# LIGHT *and* SPACE

THE TWO QUALITIES THAT SEPARATE TOWNS FROM THE COUNTRY ARE
LIGHT AND SPACE. INSTEAD OF BEING BOUND BY BUILDINGS AND ROADS,
PEOPLE CRAVE THE VAULTED SKIES OF THE OPEN FIELDS. THESE PAGES
SHOW HOW TO CREATE A FEELING OF SPACE AND LIGHT IN ROOMS
ANYWHERE.

# MODERN PASTELS

RIGHT: Blue is the colour of nature, sky and water, and represents space and well-being in many cultures. Yet, as a decorating colour, it is both sophisticated and easy on the eye – both peaceful and versatile. Here a small splash of blue adds definition.

LEFT: Watery shades of green, blue and aqua make a harmonious palette. Greens and blues are naturally close to each other, varying from lilac, lavender and turquoise to celadon and an almost greyish green. Try three of four shades of the same colour together, as seen here, to achieve a calm effect.

PASTELS TAKE THEIR INSPIRATION from spring flowers – daffodil yellows, light young greens, lilac, crocus and hyacinth blues or pale blossom pinks. They are the softest tones in the colour spectrum because they've had white added to them, turning bright reds, strong blues and greens chalky or milky. They're often considered 'safe' colours, and are used because people may feel nervous about using something brighter. But pastels can have a very distinct character of their own, and, if chosen because you really love them, can create some of the most dramatic, yet easy-to-live with, effects in decorating.

Modern pastels are ideal for making a spare, minimalist room look softer and more inviting, and they're particularly suited to the light found in the northern hemisphere. In cooler countries like Sweden, for example, pastels are traditional decorating shades, while further down south, in the hotter Mediterranean countries, much brighter colours are normally used.

LEFT: Details are important in creating the right atmosphere in a pastel scheme. Mix old and new; the chandelier is an antique, the incense block (CENTRE) was designed by Janie Jackson, and the doorknob (BOTTOM) is a modern design.

RIGHT: The impact of pastel colours can be quite intense if you use a limited number of closely related shades together.

ABOVE: Pastels are literally colour with varying amounts of white added – this is why they always look good with white, as is shown here with this painted floor.

OPPOSITE: Adding one outrageous or elaborate touch to a simple scheme adds sparkle.

## UNDERSTANDING PASTELS

TONE IS ONE OF THE important clues to understanding pastels. It relates to the depth of colour, as pastels of the same tone usually work together well. A pale chalky green sits beautifully with a pale chalky lilac, blue or tangerine, and they will all mix together to give the effect of fondant icing. If you're using a mix of patterns, such as checks, stripes and florals, then keeping them in the same tone or depth will make them look as though they belong.

However, this doesn't mean that everything in the room needs to be in the same tone, but your should use other tones – such as a vivid splash of purple, or a bright, vibrant red – in small quantities as accent colours. Otherwise, their more strident tones will drown out the delicate murmurings of your pastel shades and overwhelm the decorative scheme.

Pastels team well with white because their shades already contain white. This room has floorboards that have been painted white to reflect the light, and make a room which has only an ordinary amount of natural light seem airy and open. They are also more practical than carpeted white floors, as paint is cheaper to renew than carpet. Having the colour – a pale apple green – on the walls when the floor is painted white, also gives a nice twist to the more conventional approach, which is where colour is seen on the floor, for example, in a carpet, while the walls remain white.

The furniture is designed by Janie Jackson, and its cool, contemporary lines are softened by the delicate cushion fabrics. Soft pastel silks, with a few stronger colours shot through as a contrast, prevent the look from becoming too austere. Keeping furniture and rooms clean, and bare, while adding ornate touches, such as chandeliers, coloured door knobs and pretty cushions is a light, modern way of using colour.

# WORKING WITH WHITE

RIGHT: A central pillar in this combined room conceals a bath and shower, but leaves enough space on either side for light to flow through.

LEFT: Contemporary elements – such as modern lamps – look good when mixed with traditional furniture to achieve an effect that is relaxed yet uncluttered. Decorative accessories are all either white or in the contrast colour of green, which ensures a calm atmosphere ideal for a bedroom.

WHITE IS BOTH EASY to live with and to decorate with, but its very popularity can lead to it being a 'safe' choice. It's light and airy, calm and fresh, and most rural cultures have their standard, slightly 'soft' white paint, such as limewash, whitewash and distemper, while the brilliant whites of today are largely a modern, urban look – having that washing powder whiteness that was not invented until chemical optical brighteners were introduced to paint in the early 20th century.

White makes any space look larger and emphasizes any natural light there is in a room; and, symbolically, it stands for calm and purity. It is very flexible and 'goes' with any and every colour.

These qualities make it an ideal choice for rooms where people relax, such as bedrooms, but, to get the best effect, it still requires thought, as the down side of such flexibility is that white rooms can look ordinary.

LEFT: These decorative accessories all keep to the theme: an old mirror from a junk shop is transformed with white paint, a silver frame is a 'white' metal (CENTRE), and an old-fashioned dressing table with mirror (BOTTOM) acquires new chic when painted white.

A good solution is to take a theme, such as white-on-white, white with an accent colour (one that is used in small amounts) or white with one other colour in equal partnership (see *Blue-and-white* on pages 56–63). This bedroom is basically white-on-white, with green used as an accent colour.

## CHOOSING A CONTRAST COLOUR

GREEN IS THE COLOUR of nature, grass and fields, and represents balance, harmony and abundance in many cultures, making it a good choice for a room where calm is required, such as a bedroom. As a decorating colour, it is both sophisticated and easy on the eye, but also peaceful and versatile. This room, unusually, is a combined bedroom-and-bathroom, and colour was planned from the first piece that was found for the room – the second-hand double basin. This soft celadon green is married with pure white, and the green is echoed in a delicate leaf pattern on the bedlinen, as well as in the adjacent bathroom with the beautiful 1930s double basin that was discovered in a junk shop and re-conditioned.

Flowers and ornaments pick up the theme – it is seen in the grass-green of guelder roses and the innocent green-and-white of lilies-of-the-valley. You could, however, take your colour inspiration from a favourite vase, bedcover or bedlinen, a painting, or even the view outside the room. It's a simple but effective way of choosing a colour scheme, and one that can be achieved inexpensively.

The objects on the mantelpiece are a romantic mix of family photographs and *objets trouvés*, but there is an underlying theme of glass, metal and white that makes them all sit together in perfect harmony. The picture frames are made from cheap pine and bought in bulk from a home store chain such as IKEA, then roughly painted with white emulsion to give them a driftwood look. There's a distressed daisy mirror in a weathered frame by Janie Fox, an etched glass candlestick from Monsoon, an embroidered bedcover from an Indian market and an old-fashioned dressing table, which was also found in a junk shop and painted white. The only really extravagant touch is the green shot velvet throw which covers the bed – it is a brilliant statement of colour that truly transforms the room.

ABOVE AND LEFT: When you work in a
limited colour spectrum – here it is white
and green, with 'white' metals such as
silver and natural tones or clear glass
blending in – you can quite easily
combine traditional and modern vases,
jugs and other accessories.

LEFT AND ABOVE: In this white bedroom, the colour element – green – comes from the lavish velvet bedcover by John Rocha and an embroidered Indian throw from an inexpensive ethnic shop. The theme or colour scheme could easily be transformed quickly and inexpensively by changing the bedding and switching round a few accessories, which is another great advantage of working with the colour white.

ABOVE: Delicate pastel lampshades (LEFT) add sparkle to the scheme. Buy flannels, towels, soaps and bath crystals that echo the decorative feel (RIGHT). Subtle pastels, with a hint of grey, are more natural and less synthetic than sugar-candy shades, and partner contemporary materials well, such as weathered or 'white' metals (e.g. silver), and bleached or pale woods.

LEFT: This renovated Thirties double-basin (FAR LEFT) was found in a junk shop and inspired the colour scheme. Bathroom paraphernalia and family photographs sit side by side (TOP). Coloured photo frames work well within the scheme (CENTRE). The taps are original (BOTTOM) and have been renovated to work with modern plumbing systems.

Green married with white is sophisticated and has a feeling of fresh air. Here the kind of miscellaneous items you might find at a country auction have been made elegant by painting them all white: old gilt mirrors are now matt white, as are the French-style dressing table and picture frames. If you don't have the money to restore old bits and pieces – a lick of white paint revives them and gives a room a calm, contemporary feel.

## THE PRACTICALITIES

IF YOU WANT TO HAVE a similarly spacious bedroom-bathroom, there are certain practicalities to consider beyond the decorating theme. The advantages of combining the two rooms is that you gain light and space, but you do lose some privacy.

However, it's important to remember some essential things. Firstly, you must ensure that water and electricity never mix. Lighting and sockets must be kept well away from any water sources, and all lighting in the bathroom area must be sealed off. Never use standard lamps or pieces of electrical equipment anywhere near the bath or basin area.

Here, this centrally positioned bath has a shower, and the curved wall-cum-screen that goes around half the circular bath is extensive enough to provide all the protection that the room needs from the shower spray. Generally however, centrally placed baths cannot also have showers. Other plumbing considerations include providing some kind of slope to let the water drain away. Here, the bath has been built up slightly to allow a change of level for the water to flow away easily.

Don't compromise on fixtures and fittings, and check carefully that plumbing works. A bath in a bedroom is only luxurious when it works well – without plumbing problems.

# LIVING WITH WORK

RIGHT: A white theme looks right with white or pale grey filing cabinets, which help to keep the whole space feeling light and spacious.

LEFT: The desk top has been inexpensively made from a straight piece of wood, and open shelving holds stationery, filing and other storage boxes. Built-in drawers on the last shelf house pens, pencils, stamps and other small stationery items.

WORKING FROM HOME HAS changed people's lives today, but it is difficult to make a home office that is both efficient and looks as good as the rest of the house, as people are often reluctant to spend as much money decorating it. However, if you are spending any real amount of time working at home, then it's worth it – your productivity and sense of achievement will always be better in an enjoyable space with well-planned storage.

It's also important to make a home office a different and a more pleasant environment than one in an office block, for example. This is part of the dream of working from home. Essentially a busy space, the home office needs to be efficient, but calm and ordered.

This office, designed by Janie Jackson, has plenty of open storage, so that everything is within easy reach. The desk top is a straight piece of wood, into which has been built two filing cabinets and a set of wire drawers. Three rows of shelves run the length of the small room, and one has narrow drawers, with almost endless storage for small stationery items.

ABOVE: The vases and
bottles that line the
window sill (TOP) come
from Parma Lilac.

RIGHT: A thin 'window' cut
between the two rooms
helps to increase the light
in the office area.

ABOVE: Slim drawers under the bottom shelf (LEFT) ensure plenty of storage for small office necessities such as paper clips and pens. Good lighting is critical in home offices (CENTRE), so make sure you plan it properly. Accounts books, files and folders can all be neatly stored on the shelves (RIGHT).

## PLANNING REQUIREMENTS

BEFORE BUILDING ANY SHELVING or buying any furniture for the home office, consider the room's electrical requirements. You'll need a good working light for both day and night use. This office has opaque Perspex shutters designed by Janie Jackson to allow in maximum light while still retaining privacy. This is important for those regularly working at a computer screen, as they cut out reflective glare.

More natural light has been reclaimed by cutting a narrow, high-up 'window' between the office and the room behind it, which acts as a temporary showroom for Parma Lilac goods. This means that borrowed light from the sunnier front room helps to make the north-facing back room brighter. An angled desk light is essential, so that you can adjust the light to where it's needed. And it is important to consider how many sockets you'll need for computers, printers, or photocopiers, for example. Here, a gap has been allowed for cabling to run down the back of the desk area, to plug sockets on that wall, so that there is no chance of any electrical wiring spreading across the room and tripping people up.

## WELL-PLANNED STORAGE

STORAGE IS THE OTHER critical area to think about, and anyone setting up an office at home for the first time generally underestimates the amount of storage any business will generate in the first year. So always try to provide more storage than you think you'll need, and, if you know anyone in a similar line of work who has a home office, check with them what they need and use.

You'll need a place for your computer, fax, telephone (or two, to have a dedicated outgoing line), answering machine, filing cabinets, drawers for stationery and shelves for reference books or magazines. You can buy or build flexible modular shelf, storage and desk systems, which are easy to modify, add to, or change around as your business develops.

ABOVE: A spare room which is next to the office provides a temporary showroom for the Parma Lilac products.

LEFT: A long strip of white-painted desk offers plenty of work area but does not take up much room. The upright at the end of the desk offers useful wall space.

## DECORATING STYLE

THE BASICS OF AN OFFICE – filing cabinets, computers and printers – are not very decorative items, and the enormous volume of paperwork, samples and general clutter that most working practices generates doesn't help either. Choosing a single colour scheme or using a range of tones can create calm amongst the muddle.

In this office, the scheme is a basic white one with touches of black or dark grey as an accent. This looks smart and helps the room to seem lighter, but it is relatively easy and cheap to achieve. The filing boxes are mainly steel, which also reflect light, and there's some other filing storage in dark metallic grey. Having lots of boxes and files that look the same instantly improves and streamlines the look, so buy as many as you can initially. Styles change frequently, although these shown here are essentially office classics that will probably always be available. A laptop computer and fax answering machine in severe black fit in well in these surroundings.

As your home office is entirely yours, you can also decide to work surrounded by colour, but it's often wise to make this as flexible as possible. Painting one wall in a vivid colour (orange or purple, for example, are both considered the colours of creativity, while turquoise is supposed to stimulate new ideas) is re-vitalizing, yet relatively easy to change if you get tired of it. You can also use metal spray paints on filing cabinets (available from motor accessory shops) and use storage boxes in fashionable shades.

# OLD *and* NEW

COUNTRY TRADITIONS LAST FOR GENERATIONS, AND
PRECIOUS POSSESSIONS ARE PASSED DOWN THROUGH
THE YEARS. THE SENSE OF TIMELESSNESS THEY GIVE CAN
BE COMBINED WITH CONTEMPORARY DESIGN TO MAKE A
HOUSE REALLY FEEL LIKE A HOME.

# BAZAAR STYLE

RIGHT: Experiment when putting together different shapes and colours – this writing 'picture' by Toby Mott adds a tone of humour at a writing desk full of books and pens.

LEFT: White walls, with the palest hint of pink, make a flexible background to a scheme that is primarily defined by flashes of accent – e.g. the vibrant pinks and reds in the cushions and throw. These can be swapped for other vivid tones, such as tangerine or lime green to change the look of the room completely.

THIS L-SHAPED STUDIO ROOM in a tall, terraced house was decorated by Sam Robinson, who co-owns the cult clothing and interiors shop, The Cross, in London's Notting Hill. An eclectic, bazaar style is one of the most welcoming and vibrant ways of decorating a home, and is rooted in the traditions of classic English decorating, while retaining its own special modern twist. It is easy to think that this is a style that piles clutter on clutter, but, in fact, there are a few underlying themes that pull it all together, although they are never adhered to so slavishly that they intrude on the relaxed atmosphere.

In this room, flashes of red and vivid pink catch the eye. They're warm and welcoming colours, and yet they also make a dramatic impact. These elements – a vibrant pink picture and cushion, scarlet sofa cushions and red flowers anchor the collections, but they are also a small enough part of the scheme to be exchanged for another vivid hues – lime green, perhaps, zingy tangerine or blues and aquas – when fashions change.

LEFT: Every home has a few inherited pieces – use them to add age and character to a scheme. Here, an old linen press has been filled with clothes. Vases and cushions are collected from miscellaneous places including British cult shops: Cath Kidston, Myriad and The Cross.

## THE PALETTE

THE FIRST STEPS HERE WERE SIMPLE to achieve. The walls were painted white with a hint of pink in it to warm it up, offering the maximum flexibility to change colour and decorative schemes whenever necessary.

The floorboards had been painted by a previous owner like a chequerboard which had become very worn, but their slightly peeling effect was part of their charm so they were not altered. Shabby chic is an established style and one that works very well in an eclectic decorative mix, so always think carefully before renovating a piece of furniture. If the furniture has any value, renovation may actually reduce it. For example, restoring old silvered mirrors that have gone cloudy makes them worth less.

Sofas are also part of the background palette, because they are expensive to change. However, this can be overcome by using colourful throws and cushions.

RIGHT: There are literally no rules to this eclectic style: vases, cushions and ornaments, such as this Hawaiian doll (BOTTOM LEFT), sit side-by-side in a riot of colour.

RIGHT: The mantlepiece over the fireplace is crowded with pictures and other items that Sam Robinson has acquired, both old and new, that sit happily together.

LEFT: Mix different things that have been bought, found and made: The jugs and vases with mirrors inset are by Nicola Tassie at The Cross (TOP LEFT), a Victorian glass pendant is twined into a wall lamp (TOP RIGHT), a vintage light blends into the mix (BOTTOM LEFT) and seashells are glued around a door handle (BOTTOM RIGHT).

## A MIX OF CULTURES

EVERY SURFACE HERE IS crowded with bits and pieces from all over the world – from Chinatown in London and New York, from flea markets and fashionable boutiques, from antique shops and places which sell junk. There is a mix of old and new, cheap and expensive, handmade pieces and mass-produced items. There are no set rules, but the advice from Sam Robinson is to be as bold as possible. Her magpie eye picks things up in markets all over the world, and she is never afraid to put a stone Buddha next to a plastic Hawaiian dancer, or a faded Union Jack next to a modern painting.

'Crowding it up' is a well known decorative technique, and is when the sum is more effective than any individual parts. Crowding it up means that one or two valuable or intrinsically beautiful items are juxtaposed with less striking, but nevertheless interesting pieces to create a vibrant, welcoming scheme. There's no responsibility for any

ABOVE: The wardrobe was bought from a junk shop (RIGHT), then the doors were removed so that the clothes inside could become part of the decoration. The chest of drawers was found in a market in Kensington.

LEFT: Use small amounts of opulent fabrics, such as tiny silk cushions, big old mirrors and real candlelight to create a Bohemian and exotic look.

particular piece to be valuable or perfect, and nothing is taken too seriously – often something that would look completely inappropriate when displayed on its own can be enchanting within a group. It's enough for something to be pretty, to provide a brilliant flash of colour, to make people laugh, to remind you of a happy time, or just simply to be. This approach does away with a conventional notion of what is 'good taste' and replaces it with fun, *joie de vivre* and a sense of timelessness. It's important not to worry about being too contrived in what you do in your home, and to enjoy using kitsch as much as genuine art.

## FLORAL PATTERN

ALTHOUGH THERE ARE MANY different patterns in this room, flowers are another repeated element. They appear painted on a screen, embroidered on a throw, printed on cushions and painted on jugs and vases. There are real blooms and silk ones, little floral details and big floral statements.

Mirrors are positioned on almost every wall to reflect light, and the huge, floor-to-ceiling windows have only a thin piece of voile fabric from Warris Vianni covering them. They are just hemmed and hung, so that if a change of style is needed it will be cheap and easy to achieve. Making a bigger investment in curtains can commit you to a certain style for longer than you may want.

LEFT: The eclectic look works just as well in kitchens, where it can distract the eye from outdated fittings such as this white Seventies tap and basin.

ABOVE: Anything beautiful – or anything that you love – can be part of a decorative scheme. These slippers and bag are too colourful to hide away (CENTRE). Before completely changing a serviceable kitchen, see if altering one or two key details will update it. This kitchen is equipped with Fifties finds, such as flowered storage jars (LEFT). Such things are not genuine antiques and are still very reasonably priced in flea markets, garage or car boot sales.

## STORAGE AND DECORATION

IN ANY STUDIO FLAT, storage is always a problem and here, items of clothing, handbags, and shoes are all displayed on open shelves. They hang from rails or are even arranged on table tops as part of the decorative detail.

The wardrobe door has been removed to reveal the clothes inside. When you have pretty things, such as embroidered bags or shoes, it seems a pity not to enjoy them all the time rather than just when they're worn. However, there is a limit to what you want to see, and one good trick employed here is to send winter or summer clothes to a storage company to free up space.

At one end of the L-shape is a kitchen which contains mass-market units. By changing the wall tiling and the units' handles, and painting them white to match the rest of the room, the fact that the style was not the owner's choice was made much less important. The bathroom, too, was not renewed, but, to liven it up, thousands of pretty shells have been stuck in a border on the walls and as a feature around the door handle.

To glue shells, or other decorative items, to a wall, you'll need a good household glue, such as PVA or epoxy resin glue, both of which are available from DIY shops. Epoxy resin glue is the stronger, so always wear gloves while applying it.

If you're going to glue shells to something that's going to be used regularly, such as a door handle, make sure that they don't stick out so much that you'll graze your hand every time your turn the knob. Alternatively, you could adopt a more cautious version of the look by just gluing some shells to picture frames or mirror surrounds, rather than fixing them to walls or doors.

# ETHNIC

RIGHT: This look has no matching items, and things are not bought to go with each other or in sets, which makes for a very relaxed air of abundance in a room.

LEFT: Rich colours, such as dark green, deep royal blue or this warm, opulent red make good backgrounds to the ethnic look, making the room seem both cosy and grand, and providing a superb background for displaying a range of pictures.

THE COUNTRY HOUSE IN BRITAIN has always been filled with treasures from the East and Middle East, acquired through years of trade, dating back to the Spice Trails and Silk Routes from India in the Middle Ages. New countries, however, such as North America, were too busy establishing themselves to spend time creating decorative detail and have established more pared-down, light, airy interiors. The influence from the East is bolder and generally their opposite. As older, originally wealthier civilizations, they have established a heritage of rich colours and patterns. From the East and the Middle East come ochre, cinnabar red, black and vermilion, with fretwork carvings, intricate patterns and rich dark woods. Brilliant silks come from India, while regal colours and patterns such as gold and purple emerge from the old Moorish empire and are still found in Morocco today. Today's modern traveller, like the Aristocrat who did the Grand Tour in the 19th century, likes to bring home some enriching ethnic artefacts from their trip.

125

ABOVE: A colourful tribal hat with exotic decoration that was bought on an Eastern trip is proudly displayed in this room.

LEFT: This mantelpiece has not been 'arranged', although larger items are on the outer ends, and smaller pieces in the middle, mixing eastern and western pottery and china. In this look, the whole is more than the sum of the parts – just keep adding and taking away pieces until you like the look of it, but change it round from time to time to enjoy new pieces.

## AN INSPIRED STYLE

THE ETHNIC LOOK HAS, THEREFORE, EVOLVED as a rich, global-inspired style, mixing Indian silks with Persian carpets, Moroccan glasses, tribal throws and African artefacts in one glorious symphony. Mixing it all together isn't difficult, and once again, there are no rules, but, while the New England look relies on discipline and restraint, the ethnic style really benefits from an attitude of over-indulgence and opulence. This is the sitting room of Lucinda Chambers, who chose a white background for her rose-inspired kitchen. Here, however, she knew she wanted a strong rich colour. After considering an opulent green, she settled on this rich red, a perfect background for pictures, and a colour that is both grand and cosy. Once again, she painted large strips of several colours and took at least six months to decide on exactly the right shade. And, while the cool, pared-down interiors of some cultures look best with pale woods, such as pine, beech, elm and unstained oak, this is a look in which to use the opulent patina of the darker or mid-tone woods, such as cherrywood and mahogany.

'Ethnic' can stand for anything, from the wooden bowls of Africa to the embroidery of Middle European gypsies, but a combination of East and West, or, at the very least, a mix of cultures, is usually seen. Here, kilim cushions sit beside velvet embroidered ones, African tribal art is by a contemporary modern sketch, and lamps that were bought in the United States are on intricate Moroccan mosaic table. Lucinda changes things round constantly – she believes that a house is never 'done', or finished, and that if you enjoy finding things, then it's always worth finding somewhere to put them by altering and refining the balance in a room.

ABOVE: Twine jewellery round door handles or a bust (LEFT AND CENTRE) instead of locking it away in a jewel box. Nothing need be too new in this look: an air of age and wear adds character, as seen in these containers (RIGHT). There is no need to throw something away just because it is a bit cracked or weathered.

LEFT: Reds, pinks and browns dominate the collections found in this room: this Eastern vase is delicately etched, yet sits well with bolder pieces. Beadwork (CENTRE) is another theme found on items displayed around the room, and also on cushions. Don't be afraid of clashing colours – the pink of this rose (BOTTOM) is wonderful against the red walls. In this look, more is more – go over the top and be as daring as you want to be. Paint and accessories can easily be changed.

RIGHT: A collection of photo frames, each one different from the next, holds family photos. Flowers (FAR RIGHT) echo the warm pinks and reds of the room. This lamp (BOTTOM RIGHT) was bought in the United States, where lamp design is often more wide-ranging than in Europe. Collections of embroidery and mosaics, including this pair of boots (BOTTOM LEFT), are on display throughout.

## HOW TO BUY ABROAD

EVERYONE WILL BE FAMILIAR WITH souvenir syndrome. You go abroad, see wonderful things in the shops and markets, but when you bring them home they often look out of place. Yet people who travel frequently do often have beautiful homes, crammed full of things which act as pleasing mementoes. As one of the world's top fashion directors, Lucinda travels constantly, and her home is filled with beautiful items she has found in flea markets and shops everywhere. The old adage 'buy only what you love' – invaluable advice when buying art or antiques – stands good for buying ethnic goods abroad. If you buy to fill a gap, for example, says Lucinda, then that's when you make mistakes.

It's also important to find out a bit about what the area is best known for – rugs in Turkey and Morocco, for example, or silks in India, and ask local people, either friends or hotel staff, where the best sources are. Find time to visit without buying – simply walking round and looking at everything, and assessing prices will give you an idea of what you can get for your budget. It's a mistake to equate 'ethnic' with cheap, or to buy something because you thought you saw it back home at three times the price. Those will have been bought by a professional buyer familiar with current tastes, who makes sure that the quality is good. You may well be looking at a cheap version in the country of origin. Once you've established what a fair price is, and roughly judged a good piece, because you've seen several examples, you're better placed to buy.

Of course, the trade that was established by the Silk Routes and the Spice Trails still goes on today, and you can buy ethnic artefacts in every major world city, so buying when you return home is an option, particularly if want antiques or second-hand items. A rug, for example, could have been made in the Middle East in the 19th century, spent 100 years on a floor in Britain, and be available for sale in the US. Antiques and local artefacts regularly go from Europe to Britain, and back, or over to the US. Once again, either buy because you love the shape and colour, or find out as much as you can about the category – whether it be Delft porcelain, Venetian mirrors or Chinese lacquerwork – before buying for yourself.

# *Hidden* SANCTUARIES

CREATE A SECRET SPACE FOR YOU TO
ESCAPE FROM YOUR BUSY LIFE. HAVE A
PLACE TO ENJOY A FANTASY, OR SIMPLY
TO BE. SANCTUARIES ARE HOMES FOR
THE SOUL, WHETHER THEY'RE IN A
TINY CORNER OF A TOWN GARDEN OR
ON THE OPEN ROAD. DECORATE TO
FULFIL YOUR DREAMS; FLOWERS,
COWBOY THEMES OR TURN-OF-
THE-CENTURY COLONIAL
COLOURS ALL
WORK WELL.

# OUTDOOR RETREAT

RIGHT: The retreat, filled with wicker furniture, is built along the end of a much-loved long, thin town garden. You can easily build a summerhouse that looks as if it has been there for generations.

LEFT: Soft candlelight, a hammock and luminous cushions in Indian silk make this verandah seem part of somewhere wild and distant, rather than the middle of a city. Don't be afraid of taking accessories outside – there's no need to stick to 'proper' garden furniture.

THIS RETREAT IS MORE than just a shed at the end of a long, narrow town garden. It's an echo of the architecture from the childhood of its designer, Hazel Collins. She took the design from the verandahs of Savannah, Georgia, USA, and added on a room for peace and meditation. In the middle of city life, her aim was to feel close to nature, and also to have a special space to get away from the constant noise and bustle.

The retreat runs across the end of the garden, and two-thirds of it is a covered verandah, with the other third a small square room that is painted white. Constructed in wood that has been tongue and grooved by joiners, its style could be Edwardian, or perhaps colonial Mexican, or in fact from anywhere other than downtown London in the 21st century. There are stout hanging hooks to hold a big comfy hammock, and wicker furniture painted in happy jewel shades of blue and lilac adds to the relaxed, calm atmosphere of this special place.

RIGHT AND BELOW: The 'verandah' runs across two-thirds of the garden and is deep enough to take a dinner table and chairs for romantic dining by candlelight on summer nights. The remaining third is the adjoining 'meditation' room, painted white, which takes up the rest of the space across the garden.

## SHADY SPACE

FOR ALL ITS FEELINGS of light and sunshine, the retreat is located at the northerly end of a south-facing garden, and is also heavily overshadowed by big trees. So the little room has been painted white inside to maximize the light, and all the furniture and curtains are in bright, pastel shades, as if to echo reflected sunlight. There are Indian silks, fitting for the colonial atmosphere, which are light enough to add reflection and sparkle.

The paint on the outside of the retreat takes its hue from nature. The Berrington Blue colour, a Farrow & Ball shade, reflects the pale light of the northern skies, and fits beautifully with the natural vegetation of the abundant and much loved garden around it. Paint can seem intrusive out in the garden, but, generally speaking, the subtler the colour, and the closer to nature that it appears, the more likely it is to blend with the flowers and shrubs.

The light in the northern hemisphere, even on a sunny day, is predominantly blue, so it is the cooler blues and purples that work best in such gardens. If you want to create an outside retreat nearer to the Equator, you can use brighter colours and white, but they can look a little bleak under northern skies. Under a soft, grey sky, subtle blues and purples will look rich, oranges and warm yellows will look warm under almost any sky, and earth colours will work everywhere from the southern hemisphere to Greece, the Middle East, Mediterranean France and northern Europe. Bright colours can be brought in as spot colour, such as in cushions, which can be taken outside on a sunny day and hastily retrieved when the sky clouds over and their colours seem to become harsh and tawdry.

ABOVE: Wicker furniture is inexpensive to buy, and can be painted or dressed up in silk and velvet. There is a very contemporary mix of ancient and modern, and of East and West on the verandah: the china accessories and wicker furniture are Victorian, but the cool, uncluttered way they are presented is very modern. The luxurious cushions are made from Indian silk.

RIGHT: Graceful lilies and the glow of several candles adds to the atmosphere for evening dining in this outdoor retreat. Use lots of candles, but protect them by using glass shades, or dropping nightlights into glasses or jam jars (but never leave them unattended).

# GYPSY CARAVAN

RIGHT: A sanctuary can be portable or mobile; park a caravan at the end of a town garden or on the beach for dreams of the open road. The detailing on this caravan is exquisite, with gilding featuring extensively.

LEFT: A Victorian gypsy caravan which has been faithfully restored and repainted in its original colours. When the gypsies who originally lived in these caravans earned extra money, they invested it in their mobile home by adding fine gilding, elaborate paintwork. panelling and fretwork. This was because they had no other home to maintain, they did not use banks, and there was very little else to spend it on.

THE COMPACT PRETTINESS of a gypsy caravan evokes memories of country holidays meandering along lanes bordered with wild flowers, camping in woody glades and cooking over a log fire. But like the Airstream (see pages 144–151), the gypsy caravan is a mobile dream, and can be transported anywhere you want; it will also create a quiet corner at the bottom of the garden, and offer a taste of life outside the fast lane.

The gypsies who originally lived in these caravans were nomadic people, and they moved from place to place doing tinkering or farm work according to the season. Each caravan is a complete miniature home with a double bed-cum-seat at the back, where parents and young babies slept, a stove at the side with a mantelpiece and mirror on top, and little cupboards and an area beneath the bed for essential storage. Older children were expected to sleep under the caravan until they got old enough to earn money to buy their own caravan.

ABOVE AND LEFT: To achieve a relaxed, cottage-like look, don't match patterns. Here each cushion is different. Using a whole range of reds – from bright pinks to scarlet, poppy and berry reds – is a successful way of working with one colour. Yellow, red and white are the only three colours used. Limiting the number of colours looks very contemporary.

RIGHT: Use floral fabrics which have lots of white in their backgrounds to help keep an atmosphere light and airy. Add extra touches like the bobble trim on the voile, and bring in a few scraps of antique fabric, such as the old blue French quilt.

ABOVE: An iron lighting sconce for candles bought from an antique shop when the caravan was being restored.

BELOW: The fine paintwork and gilding on this door handle (LEFT) and door (RIGHT) have been faithfully restored. A traditional Kelly kettle (CENTRE) has a separate compartment in which dried twigs are placed and lit to heat the water quickly and efficiently. Touches like these add authenticity to a scheme.

But it is the gypsy decorative theme that most people are drawn to, and it's a look that is perfect for furnishing bedrooms, little girl's rooms and even cottage-like living rooms. The casual way that scraps of material are sewn together to make light curtains is the key to the overall look, along with the combination of a variety of floral patterns. Each cushion in this caravan is made from a different fabric. The way they have been put together shows that almost anything goes – vivid modern magenta pinks sit side-by-side with deep Victorian maroon, and spriggy patterns harmonize with checks and stripes. The way to achieving a relaxed look that seems to have evolved over the years is to avoid matching fabrics. So while some of the spriggy florals on white backgrounds look quite similar, they are all quite different close up.

## HOW TO MIX PATTERNS

THE KEY TO THIS LOOK is that there is some unity of colour. If you look carefully, you'll see that there is an overall theme of yellow and red – albeit an entire range of yellows and reds from palest cream to magenta pinks. Many interior decorators today work with just two or three colours in a room to get an effect that looks relaxed but contemporary. Here the three colours are red and yellow, with blue being added as an accent colour, which is seen in flashes in the antique chair and the rug on the bed. This interior theme echoes the colours of the caravan, which is painted deep maroon with buttery yellow walls. So, when choosing a colour scheme, whether for a gypsy caravan or a town sitting room, this approach of keeping to two basic colours makes a scheme look modern.

## WORKING WITHIN ONE COLOUR

THE USE OF COLOUR IN THIS CARAVAN also illustrates another good way of working with colour, which is to take a limited number of colours (perhaps even just one, such as

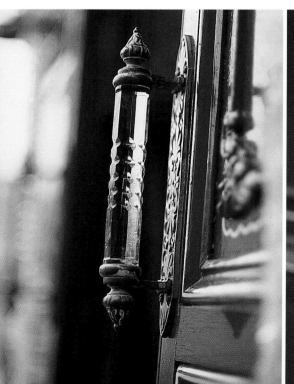

red), but to use the entire spectrum, from candyfloss pinks, classic red ginghams, berry reds to deep maroon. It is interesting to note that if you put two different reds – or two different blues, or greens – together, they may clash, but if you add other shades and tones of red (or blue, or green, depending on which colour you're working with), then the whole look acquires a unity, and has a depth and vividness that couldn't be achieved in any other way. It's a popular interior decorator trick to blend four or five different tones of the same colour to make a colour scheme look lively and natural.

## How to lighten up

USING STRONG COLOUR in a small space is a good way of making it seem cosy and welcoming. In the tiny confines of this caravan's interior, it would have been pointless to paint it white to try and make it look bigger or lighter. However, white does have its uses in keeping everything light and airy, and here it has been used extensively in the background of the fabrics, and in the curtains hanging at the window. If you think a scheme is beginning to look too muddled or heavy, try the trick of adding white – perhaps a white muslin curtain at the window, or cushions with a white background to change the look.

ABOVE: The stove (LEFT), although not originally fitted in the caravan, is a Victorian one of a similar type. It is in full working order, and is regularly used for cooking food. The Victorian mantelpiece (RIGHT), complete with mirrors, helps to add to its appearance as a miniature mansion on wheels.

# AIRSTREAM

RIGHT: A caravan can be a mobile spare room, a holiday home – here this Airstream is parked on Camber Sands in Britain – or it can be placed in a town garden to act as a fantasy hideaway.

LEFT: Set the scene for a specific theme with fabrics and accessories. Here, red curtains and a Stars and Stripes bedspread are combined to create a Wild West look.

SECRET HIDEAWAYS don't have to be fixed in one place – in fact, to be able to take off, or even, perhaps, just to be able to dream of taking off one day, is sometimes all that you need to create the illusion of escape. This Fifties Airstream caravan evokes the freedom of the open road, the age of Jack Kerouac and the endless arid miles of the Arizona desert in the USA. But, when not mobile, and parked at the end of a town garden, it can act as an office, special hideaway, or even a spare bedroom for guests. When it is driven away for the holidays, the caravan can become a portable bedroom for visiting friends.

## RETRO STYLE

AN AIRSTREAM IS A particularly stylish retro caravan, but it illustrates how you can furnish a dream even in small spaces. The countryside evoked here is in the style of the Wild West, but any culture or theme where travel and exploration is a way of life –

LEFT: In a small living space, one or two distinctive items really add to the atmosphere. This Fifties lamp was discovered in a second-hand shop. Cushions can help to make the most of your theme: here a Wild West design from Cath Kidston (BOTTOM) adds a cheerful note to the U-shaped banquettes. These act as seating by day, while at night two mattresses are added to create a huge bed, so that the Airstream can sleep two adults and three children.

RIGHT: This Formica-topped table evokes the Fifties style. It is a design that is still manufactured today, and it neatly folds up when the banquettes are used as a bed.

like the Middle-Eastern Bedouins or a circus – could be adapted for caravan decor by using accessories and fabrics. Because of restricted space only small amounts of accessorizing would be necessary.

But if you want something very specific, such as an Airstream, how do you go about acquiring one? The starting point for any specialist interest now has to be the Internet, particularly as sellers may be scattered all over the world. When photographer Simon Brown first acquired access to the Internet, he decided to look up topics he was interested in, and, remembering the lure of the desert adventures in the National Geographic magazines of his childhood, he tapped into the world of the Airstream fan. He soon found that a model, owned by an elderly blues drummer who had played with Elvis Presley, was for sale in the United States.

When you have found your model, it then has to be shipped, and, although legislation and costs vary from country to country, it is usually surprisingly affordable – although of course it does all add to your final bill. Check what the options and costs are before signing the cheque. In this case, the shipping amounted to about seven per cent of the price.

Once the Airstream had been shipped over to London in Britain, Simon Brown found its lovingly cared-for and perfectly preserved Fifties fittings needed little alteration, but some repairs were needed to make it roadworthy. If you're intending to take a caravan out on the road, this is another expense to be considered.

As a second home, albeit a mobile one, there is plenty of opportunity to have fun with decorating the interior. Kitsch, 'trailer-trash' glamour, turning the inside into a tent, or following a space-age theme and doing everything in steel and tin are all interesting options.

ABOVE: Plastics today are fun, smart and inexpensive. Colourful tableware suits the atmosphere. Here, bright, graphic plastic plates from Jerry's Home Store, gingham tea towels and decorative floral glassware have been used.

OPPOSITE: The interiors of caravans and yachts are a lesson in small-scale living, and anyone planning a tiny flat would do well to visit a yacht or caravan exhibition to pick up storage ideas. This was the original teak chest of drawers fitted to the Airstream, but Simon Brown removed the top drawer to inset a hob that could be used for cooking.

Here the Wild West theme is carried out almost entirely with accessories and fabrics, including the bedlinen, other soft furnishings and one or two amusing additions, such as a lamp with spurs. You don't need to spend much money or time to achieve a look that makes quite a visual impact.

ABOVE: The Airstream lives in the city but makes frequent visits to the country and the seaside.

## COMPACT FITTINGS

CARAVAN INTERIORS, like yacht interiors, are a lesson in compact living, and anyone trying to plan a tiny kitchen in a small flat would do well to visit a caravan or yacht show to pick up ideas for storage, food preparation and the general planning of an efficient layout. Inside the Airstream, there is a double bed, an Elsan toilet and a shower. There is also U-shaped seating and a formica table on one side, plus a chest of drawers with a hob on top, offering both cooking and storage facilities.

Everything is beautifully compact – the table folds up and two extra mattresses can then be pulled out to turn the U-shaped seating into a massive bed for several children or adults. On the other side of this caravan, an awning can be rolled out to make a relaxing place to sit and watch the sun go down. Gingham curtains, a Stars and Stripes bedspread and cushions with a Wild West theme from designer Cath Kidston complete the look, along with plates in bold, graphic colours from Jerry's Home Store.

RIGHT: The rear view of the Airstream. Metal mesh screens keep out annoying mosquitoes and other insects when the windows are open.

# DIRECTORY

Some of the furniture, lighting, bedding, china and accessories came from the following shops. As stock changes regularly, we have not listed exactly what came from where, but anyone who loves the looks on these pages will enjoy a visit to any of the shops below. Their addresses or contact numbers are in the directory, along with a number of other shops whose style is both contemporary and decorative.

## Antiques and Antique Markets

Antiques Trades Gazette
Listing of antiques auctions around the UK
020 7420 6600
www.antiquestradegazette.com

BADA (British Antique Dealers Association)
020 7589 4128
List of registered antique dealers who abide by a code of practice, also advice on buying antiques and general information.
www.bada.org

Bermondsey (New Caledonian) Antique Market
Fridays 5am–2pm
Bermondsey Square, London SE1
General antique and flea market with wide range of items

LAPADA (London & Provincial Antique Dealers Association)
List of registered antique dealers who abide by a code of practice.
020 7823 3511
www.lapada.co.uk

Myriad Antiques
131 Portland Road
London W11
020 7229 1709

Portobello Road Market
Portobello Road
London W11
Saturdays 6am–4pm
Antique and flea market with wide range of items

## Chandeliers and Lighting

Beaumont & Fletcher
261 Fulham Road
London SW3 6HY
020 7352 5553
Hand-carved lights based on historic originals

McCloud & Co
269 Wandsworth Bridge Road
London SW6 2TX
020 7371 7151
Unusual gilt and hand-painted chandeliers, lamps and sconces

Richard Taylor Designs
Southbank Business Centre
Battersea Park Road
London SW11
020 7720 2772
Wrought iron chandeliers in oak leaf, bamboo and other designs, also decorative wall lights and lamp brasses

Tindle
162–168 Wandsworth Bridge Road
London SW6 2UQ
020 7384 1485
Candlestick and other classic lamps, chandeliers

## China, Glass and Accessories

Bombay Duck
Mail order only
020 8749 8001
Decorative home accessories and wrought iron furniture

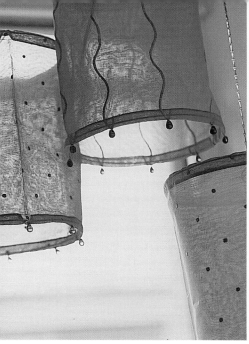

THE CROSS
141 Portland Road
London W11 4LW
020 7727 6760
www.thecrosscatalogue.com
Decorative accessories and fashion

EMMA BERNHARD
301 Portobello Road
London W10 3TE
020 8960 2929
Plastic kitchen accessories

GRAHAM & GREENE
4 Elgin Crescent
London W11
020 7727 4594
www.grahamandgreene.co.uk

KITCHENSYNC
Mail order only 020 7720 1609
Kitsch accessories

MONSOON HOME
33c Kings Road
London SW3 4LX
020 7313 3046 for nationwide stockists
www.monsoon.co.uk
Accessories and bedlinen sourced from
    countries around the world, especially
    ethnic styles from India

THE SHAKER SHOP
322 Kings Road
London SW3
020 7352 3918
www.shaker.co.uk
Shaker-style accessories

THOMAS GOODE
19 South Audley Street
London W1Y 6BN
020 7499 2823
www.thomasgoode.co.uk
Exceptionally wide range of fine
    china and glass

JERRY'S HOME STORE
163 Fulham Road
London SW3
020 7581 0909
China, glass, kitchenware and gifts with
    a classic or American theme

## FLORAL, CLASSIC AND CONTEMPORARY FABRICS AND BEDLINEN

*All stockists offer mail order unless 'No mail
    order' is specified*

LAURA ASHLEY
Stores in UK and elsewhere
Call 0875 5622116 for nearest store
Call 0800 868100 for mail order catalogue
Contemporary, floral and classic furnishing
    fabrics and fashion

BEAUMONT & FLETCHER
261 Fulham Road
London SW3 6HY
020 7352 5594
Historical, 'tea-stained' linens, chenilles and
    fine wools

BENNISON FABRICS
16 Holbein Place
London SW1W 8NL
020 7730 8076 for retail outlets
Historical 'tea-stained' floral linens in
    18th/19th century designs

COUVERTURE
310 Kings Road
London SW3 5UH
020 7795 1200
Bedlinen

DESIGNERS' GUILD
277 King's Road
London SW3
020 7351 5775
Catalogue 0845 6021189
Fabrics, wallpapers, bedlinen and accessories
    in contemporary designs

EARTH TONES
020 8345 0333
Mail order catalogue for several
    contemporary designers, ranging from
    Melin Tregwynt rugs and blankets to
    VV Rouleaux ribbons and accessories

MULBERRY HOME
41–42 New Bond Street
London W1Y 9HB
020 7491 3900 for stockists
www.mulberry-england.co.uk
Classic 'English country house' fabrics and
    accessories with a modern twist

OSBORNE & LITTLE
(also the Liberty range of fabrics)
304–308 Kings Road
London SW3 5UH
020 7352 1456
www.osborneandlittle.com
Contemporary and traditional fabrics and
    wallpapers

SANDERSON
01895 201509 for stores in the UK
www.sanderson-uk.com
Fabrics and soft furnishings in classic and
    floral patterns
No mail order

TOAST
Mail order only
01558 668800
Bedlinen, cotton pyjamas and casual clothes

THE WHITE COMPANY
Mail order only
0870 160160
White bedlinen, towels and china

## FLOORING & RUGS

*All stockists offer mail order unless 'No mail
order' is specified*

CRUCIAL TRADING
The Market Hall
Craven Arms
Shropshire SY7 9NY
01588 673666
www.original-seagrass.co.uk
Natural floorcoverings such as seagrasss,
    sisal and wool

CHRISTOPHER FARR
115 Regents Park Road
London NW1 8UR
020 7916 7690
www.cfarr.co.uk
Handmade contemporary and designer rugs

FIRED EARTH
Twyford Mill
Oxford Road
Adderbury
Oxon OX17 3HP
01295 812088
www.firedearth.com
Kilims, dhurries, floor tiles

THE RUG COMPANY
103 Lot's Road
London SW10
020 7352 0012
www.rugcompany.co.uk
Classic, contemporary and ethnic rugs

## FURNITURE

BOMBAY DUCK
Mail order only
020 8749 8001
Wrought iron furniture

THE HOLDING COMPANY
Mail order only
020 7610 9160
Storage furniture and accessories

PARMA LILAC
020 8960 9239
Contemporary furniture and accessories
designed and sourced by Janie Jackson

THE PIER
Mail order 020 7814 5004
Stores 020 7814 5020
Stores around the UK
Modern furniture and accessories

SASHA WADDELL
269 Wandsworth Bridge Road
London SW6 2TX
020 7736 0766
Swedish-style furniture and accessories

THE SHAKER SHOP
322 Kings Road
London SW3
020 7352 3918
www.shaker.co.uk

SOFA WORKSHOP
01798 343400
Mail order sofas and armchairs

VIADUCT
1–10 Sumner Street
London EC1R 5DB
020 7278 8456
www.viaduct.co.uk
Modern classics: Driade, Philippe Starck
and others

## GENERAL STORES: BUDGET AND DIY

THE HOME PLACE
26–40 Kensington High Street
London W84 4PF
020 7937 2626
Well priced general accessories such as
bedding, lighting and china
No mail order

HOMEBASE
0845 9801800 for stores in the UK
www.homebase.co.uk
DIY shop, storage, bathroom, lighting and
kitchen fittings

IKEA
020 8208 5600 for stores in the UK
Swedish furniture group known for its well
priced contemporary self-assembly furniture
Catalogue and some mail order deliveries

SHELFSTORE
6/8 Frognal Parade
158 Finchley Road
London NW3 5HH
020 7794 0313
www.shelfstore.co.uk
Kid's bedrooms, home offices and general
storage units made from interlocking
systems

## GENERAL STORES FOR A WIDE RANGE OF FURNITURE, LIGHTING, BEDDING AND HOME ACCESSORIES

THE CONRAN SHOP
Michelin House
81 Fulham Road
London SW3 6RD
www.conran.co.uk
No formal mail order but will post
specific items

HABITAT
020 72552545 for stores in the UK
www.habitat.co.uk

HEAL'S
196 Tottenham Court Road
London W1P 9LD
020 7636 1666
www.heals.co.uk
Furniture, storage, lighting, tableware,
    kitchen accessories, and bedlinen

HOUSE OF FRASER
020 7963 2236 for stores in the UK
www.houseoffraser.co.uk

SELFRIDGES
400 Oxford Street
London W1A 1AB
020 7629 1234
www.selfridges.com
No mail order

## PAINTS

*All stockists offer mail order unless 'No mail order' is specified*

BRATS
281 King's Road
London SW3 5EW
www.brats.co.uk
'Mediterranean' palette of bright, clear hues
    which can be diluted or mixed with water
    for a softer effect.

DULUX
Retail advice centre and stockists:
    01753 550555
Major paint manufacturer with wide range
    of paints

FARROW & BALL
33 Uddens Trading Estate
Wimborne
Dorset BH21 7NL
01202 876141
www.farrow-ball.com
Manufacturers of historic paints, including
    the National Trust range

FIRED EARTH
Twyford Mill
Oxford Road
Adderbury
Oxon OX17 3HP
01295 812088
Historic paints including the vivid Pugin
    colours and Kelly Hoppen neutrals

JOHN OLIVER
33 Pembridge Road
London W11 3HG
020 7727 3735
www.johnoliver.co.uk
Known for rich and vibrant colours
    and historic shades. Handpainted
    swatches supplied

PAPERS AND PAINTS
4 Park Walk
London SW10 OAD
020 7352 8626
http://sites.netscape.net/colourman/homepage
Catalogues: historic paints – £10;
    traditional – £8; off-whites – £3

# ACKNOWLEDGEMENTS

THANK YOU TO:

Cath Kidston, Laura Ashley, Sanderson, The Cross, The Shaker Shop, Graham & Greene, The White Company, Bombay Duck, Toast, Emma Bernhard, Thomas Goode, Couverture, Jerry's Home Store, Osborne & Little, Designers' Guild, Parma Lilac, Monsoon Home and The Rug Company.

We'd like to thank the friends who have generously allowed us to photograph their homes and benefit from their inspiration. Many of the ideas in this book are the result of their creativity.

# INDEX